WHAT IF GOD'S A BULLOCK?

WHAT IF GOD'S A BULLOCK?

Angela E. Lord

UNITED WRITERS
Cornwall

UNITED WRITERS PUBLICATIONS LTD
Ailsa, Castle Gate, Penzance, Cornwall.

British Library Cataloguing in Publication Data:
A catalogue record for this book is
available from the British Library.

ISBN 1 85200 110 0

Printed in Great Britain by
United Writers Publications Ltd
Cornwall.

To my dear husband Chris for all his support.
To my children, Claire and Philip
and my brothers, Malcolm and Ian.
I would also like to include Albert White
whose friendship I greatly value.

Foreword

This book is a compilation of amusing true stories that have featured in my life, revolving around people from all walks of life.

I was born and brought up in the parish of Crayford in the County of Kent.

In 1981 I moved with my husband and children to Devon where I ran a restaurant for three and a half years in Budleigh Salterton.

On moving to the village of Horrabridge, near Yelverton, in 1985, I worked as a Court Usher at Tavistock and Okehampton Magistrates' Courts for fifteen years.

In addition to my Court duties, I realised a life-long ambition; embarking on a life of self-sufficiency by setting up a smallholding which I continue to run to this day.

Chapter One

There were seven of us in the family. My parents Harold and Minnie Saxton, my maternal grandmother Elizabeth Malloy, her daughter Milbra Brooks, and my brothers Ian, Malcolm and me.

As with the best regulated of families, there were occasional arguments, but on the whole we got on well and were a very united family. I feel privileged at having come from such a close-knit family as so many children nowadays come from broken homes with catastrophic results.

My grandmother had five children, four girls and one boy, from her first marriage. Her husband had been a Civil Engineer, moving around the country working mainly on road construction. As a consequence none of her children were born in the same area and hailed from between Land's End and John o'Groats.

Her son Edward married and moved away, as did her eldest daughter Nancy. However, my mother and her two other sisters, Milbra and Irene, remained close by, Milbra living with us, and Rene, as she was known, living with her husband, William Hoadley, a short distance away.

Gran's husband, Harry Brooks, died from pneumonia at the age of forty-six. She then married an Irishman by the name of Paddy Malloy, which I believe she had reason to regret as he had a love of alcohol and slurped his way through all of her savings. However, he too was to die of pneumonia, and from then on Gran lived with my mother and father, together with Milbra, or Aunt

Cis as she was affectionately known.

We lived in a terraced house in Whitehill Road, Crayford in Kent not far from Vickers Armstrong's where my father worked during the war. Vickers was a large, depressing looking factory where munitions were manufactured for the war effort, keeping a large number of local people in employment. A whistle would blow at one o'clock when everyone would stop for lunch, and Dad would come home on his Francis Barnett motorcycle.

Our garden extended down to the railway line which was on the main line to London, and provided my brothers and I with hours of pleasure waving to the drivers of the big old locomotives as they went by, invariably leaving black smuts on the washing, which, on a particularly bad day would have to be done all over again. This was no mean feat in those days before it was the norm to have a washing machine, and meant slaving over a Belfast sink, and poking and prodding the washing that was boiling in the big copper with an old wooden rolling pin. The house would be filled with steam and bad tempers, especially if the copper boiled over, swamping the floor. Having been washed and wrung out, it would then have to be put through the mangle which lived at the foot of the back steps.

Malcolm used to play with Brian Shadbolt who lived next door, and greatly admired Brian's stone throwing ability. Brian could hit the metal fence beyond the railway line from his back step, which was a considerable achievement considering that the length of the gardens were 130 feet.

His favourite pastime was bouncing stones off the roof of the freight train that passed by during the morning. In those days trains ran strictly to time, so Brian knew precisely when to position himself on the back step with his cache of stones. On one particular occasion, Brian was to select a large stone that he ceremoniously polished on the leg of his short trousers whilst he waited in anticipation.

Mr Hopper lived next door to the Shadbolt's. He was a keen gardener with raised beds planted in neat rows with a selection of vegetables. Narrow paths wended their way between and around the beds along which Mr Hopper would walk every morning on his bowed legs, closely followed by his dog. Not a weed was to be seen, and all unwanted, winged insects were sprayed from a little metal can that seemed to be permanently in his hand. Various pellets and powders were sprinkled liberally on the ground committing anything that crawled to certain death.

As Brian awaited the arrival of the freight train, Mr Hopper was stooping down, his left arm resting on his left thigh, whilst he pulled up a weed that had had the audacity to grow in his garden. The railway signal clicked into the upward position, thus alerting Brian to the oncoming target, the train's whistle blew, and the locomotive came trundling along the track. Brian took aim, and just as the stone left his fist, Mr Hopper, clutching the weed, abruptly stood up. A resounding thud was heard as the stone made contact with the back of Mr Hopper's head. Malcolm and Brian stood staring in horror as Mr Hopper, after a pregnant pause, bellowed out a word. The word was directed at Brian, and seemed to come from the very depths of his being. The two boys fled into their respective houses where Malcolm repeated 'the word' to my mother, enquiring as to what it meant. For reply he received a hearty smack round the head, and was told never to say it again.

Not long after this unfortunate incident, Mr Hopper was to use 'the word' again.

Blackie was Mr Hopper's dog. He would not have been a contender for Cruft's, but nonetheless, was a lovely dog, and very obedient to Mr Hopper's commands. Blackie knew that the garden was sacrosanct, and on meandering along the little pathways never put a paw out of place. However, on this occasion something must have clicked in his brain and he went berserk. Onions, carrots, swedes and lettuces went flying in all directions, and the neat, manicured lawned area was strewn with dirt from Blackie's manic digging.

My mother had been pegging out the washing, giving her a grandstand view of the dog's escapade. She dropped whatever was in her hand and ran indoors, her hands clasped over her mouth, before collapsing with laughter.

Aunt Rene and Uncle Will spent quite a lot of time at our house, particularly as Uncle Will was the Manager of the Co-op along the Dartford Road, and used to walk home at lunch-time to have his meal with us.

Aunt Rene worked part-time for a bookmaker in Dartford, but was a trained shorthand typist. Prior to working for Charles Robbins the bookmaker, she was secretary to a Mr Young, a builder whose yard was located a short distance away from where she and Uncle Will lived in Dartford Road.

Mr Young's retirement forced her to change jobs, and she seemed to enjoy working for Charlie and could work out bets in a flash.

Unlike Mr Young, Charlie Robbins was quite a colourful character and used a lot of swear words that he practised on a daily basis, particularly when an 'outsider' won a race.

Initially his vocabulary shocked Aunt Rene, but she soon became accustomed to it, and was to hear every conceivable expletive known to man when Del Shannon, the pop singer, brought out a record entitled *Runaway*.

This record was extremely popular, particularly with the window cleaner who cleaned the windows of the betting shop.

Part of the lyrics went as follows:

"I wonder, I wah wah wah wah wonder,
Why, wah wah wah wah why she went away,
My little run run run run runaway."

This appeared to be the window cleaner's favourite part of the song, and he sung it at the top of his voice repeatedly until Charlie could stand no more. He went outside and, using his command of the Anglo Saxon to full effect, told him what would happen if he continued with his rendition.

My brother, Malcolm, was ten years older than me, and Ian was eighteen months my senior, making me the baby of the family, which I vehemently resented. My brothers would tease and torment me mercilessly as elder brothers are inclined to do to their little sisters, and in addition I would be used for wrestling practice. If I was not being held in a half nelson, I would be on the wrong end of an Irish whip. All very unpleasant, but it made me quite tough and able to hold my own when confronted with the school bullies.

However, as I was accustomed to walking in my sleep, I got my revenge by frightening them in the dead of night. I would do most peculiar things by all accounts, but on occasions I would simply stand over a sleeping member of the family and stare at them. Apparently my eyes would be wide open and my face deathly white, giving the recipient of my visitation a very nasty scare.

When Ian and I retired to bed, he used to plead with me not to go into his room, as he was easily frightened at the best of times, and hoped his pleas would somehow react on my subconscious mind and divert me into another direction.

When a local 'yobo' threw a neighbour's garden ornaments through his bedroom window one night, he thought his last hour had come. Initially he assumed that it was me, but as it turned out it was Snow White and three dwarfs!

My father used to get quite annoyed at having his sleep disturbed, and on nights when I had been up and about three times or more he would be tired and irritable the next morning.

One evening a programme was on the television featuring 'gymslip mothers'. My mother remarked at how sad it was and how upset she would be if I was ever to be placed in that situation. My father quickly reassured her by saying, with as much venom as a Benzedrine Puff Adder, that no one in their right mind would sleep with me.

I think this remark was made the night after I had gone to the shed at the bottom of our garden, collected my pony's saddle and thrown it over father's sleeping torso, telling him that I was going to take him out for a ride.

On one occasion, following several disturbed nights in succession, I was marched into our doctor's surgery on West Hill in the hope that a cure could be prescribed. Dr Thompson advised my mother not to feed me cheese, and the suggestion was made that a wet towel be placed beside my bed that would theoretically wake me up when I stood on it.

These measures proved to be unsuccessful, and I continued

performing my nocturnal antics, causing much annoyance and concern.

This problem was to dog me into adult life, and on one occasion, when our son was a toddler, I leapt out of bed insisting that a barrage balloon was on the ceiling. Having got me reassured and back to bed, my husband Chris then had to attend to our son who had started to scream. It transpired that he had a crocodile under his cot!

Dad was a very talented musician taking after his mother's side of the family, all of whom were musical. He was a violinist, and had played with the BBC Light Orchestra. He was also a member of a local band known as the Sid Ryder Band, and would play in the Grandstand in Dartford Park on Sunday afternoons throughout the summer months. He was an upholsterer by trade, and as a result had enormous hands, but despite the size of his fingers he could make a violin 'talk'.

For many years he worked in Bexley Hospital, our local lunatic asylum, making horse-hair mattresses, curtains and furniture. He was a very talented man, and his abilities knew no bounds. He had little or no faith in garages, and would do all his own motor repairs, thinking nothing of stripping down the engine of our car and putting it back together again.

On one occasion he had a problem with the brakes and enlisted my mother's help when it came to the point where they had to be bled. My mother, like most women, was clueless when it came to car mechanics, and had never heard of a 'bleeder' screw. When Dad told her to turn the bleeder, to his astonishment she became absolutely livid, and told him that if he was going to use that sort of language she was going indoors.

Dad's cars were usually big, old Austins. As there were seven of us to transport he had to have a large vehicle. Malcolm used to sit in the front beside Dad, I sat on Mum's lap, Ian sat on Gran's lap, and Aunt Cis, who always seemed to draw the short straw, sat on a little stool that was squeezed in front of the back seat. She would exclaim, "Oh, mother," if we went round a particularly tight bend, and did not relish the annual trips to the West Country when she would have to balance on her stool for in excess of seven hours.

Once Dad had a car that had a tear in the headlining coupled with a leaky sun roof which was bad news on wet days. On one of our trips out it poured with rain and water started to drip in through the roof. Aunt Cis laughed her head off as we all seemed to be getting wet except for her. This was not to last. The rain became torrential, the headlining came down completely, and Aunt Cis was like a drowned rat.

Dad used Farriger's Garage in Crayford to get petrol for the car. The attendant would put the fuel in and then set about cleaning the windscreen and check the oil, all as part of the service.

Our journeys never seemed to go without incident. A common problem was the engine overheating on steep hills. Yarcombe Hill was always a nightmare for Dad, and in those days you had to negotiate this hill to get into Devon. He would rest the car at the bottom, and then about halfway up we would begin to see the dreaded steam arising from under the bonnet. Pulling into the lay-by that contained cars with the same problem, we would have to wait for it to cool down before topping up with water that we always carried for the purpose in a lemonade bottle in the boot, and then proceed to the top of the hill when we would have to stop again and repeat the procedure. At least it gave Aunt Cis a chance to get off her stool and stretch her legs, if nothing else.

Malcolm was very like Dad in as much as not only was he an accomplished pianist and organist, he shared our father's love of motor cars. He bought his first car soon after passing his test when he was eighteen. It was a Morris 8, green with black mudguards.

I have never laughed so much in my life. I suppose I had been so used to Dad's enormous vehicles into which all seven of us would cram, that seeing this tiny car struck me as hilarious, especially as at this time my father owned a Hudson Terraplane which dwarfed Malcolm's car which was parked just behind.

The Morris 8 had travelled far and long, and by the time

Malcolm came in possession of it, it was on its last legs. However, my brother was absolutely beside himself with excitement, and gave no thought as to its reliability whatsoever.

Malcolm's current girlfriend was a schoolteacher who was three years his senior called Joan. She had been expecting to receive an engagement ring on the strength of the money Malcolm had spent on the car. Needless to say, his euphoria was short-lived when he came face to face with her father. A five-mile radius of Joan's house became a no-go area for Malcolm!

Driving was Malcolm's passion, getting his hands dirty was not, hence the car did not see so much as an oily rag, and it was not long before it conked out. Dear old Dad was summoned to his rescue, and discovered that the cause of the problem was the fact that the engine was dry of oil. Malcolm received a long lecture and was told not to let it happen again.

The next time it broke down, Dad was summoned once again and, with the previous episode still fresh in his mind, crawled beneath the little car and undid the screw to check for oil which he felt quite sure he would not strike. Very unfortunately for Dad on this occasion lack of oil was not the problem, and he emerged as black as the ace of spades with only the whites of his eyes showing. What followed is unprintable.

As Malcolm worked his way through various saloon cars he became besotted with more sporty little numbers, and acquired an Austin Healy Frogeye Sprite. My mother was going into Dartford one day and Malcolm volunteered to take her in the Sprite. He had been keen to give us all a ride in his prized vehicle, but Mum was not enthusiastic and had declined previous offers as the car was small and slung low to the ground, and mother was tall, well built, and not as agile as she used to be. However, on this occasion, being pressed for time, she accepted the lift.

She tried placing her posterior in first, but could not then get her legs up. Then she put her left leg in, which left her facing the wrong way. Malcolm became exasperated, told her to put her right leg in, and then pushed her down into the seat, slamming the door before she fell out.

They had an uneventful journey into the town, albeit with the engine sounding a bit rough, but on arrival the problem then arose as to how to get Mum out. She ended up on all fours crawling across the pavement.

All the while Malcolm drove clapped out old vehicles, Dad never ventured up to bed until he was home safe and sound, and always kept a can of oil and a tow-rope in the boot of his car.

My brother Ian, had to be kept under constant surveillance due to his love of getting up to mischief. Setting fire to the dining-room curtains with his Mamod steam engine, and putting a firework in the fire, causing an avalanche of soot to devastate the front room which was reserved for the doctor and vicar, to name but two of Ian's misdemeanours.

My parents guessed that they were to have problems with their second son when, at the age of eighteen months, he toddled at high speed across the beach at Eastbourne and took a towel that was providing cover for a lady who had just removed her bathing costume.

Ian was fascinated by fire, and often sported singed hair and eyebrows as a result of conducting various experiments. Warming torch batteries in the hearth to see if they would last a bit longer and then plastering the walls in tar as they exploded was a mere inconvenience when compared to the havoc he wreaked with my celluloid doll when he was keen to see how celluloid and fire would react.

Topsy went up the chimney like a rocket, only to return with a large quantity of soot. She shot up the chimney again with the same result. This horrific state of affairs was not to cease until Topsy had ascended and descended twice more before she melted, thus bringing this dreadful experiment to an end.

Fireworks were like a magnet to Ian, and he would live for Guy Fawkes' night. On one occasion we made a guy using a pair of Dad's old trousers and a threadbare jacket. We stuffed the garments with newspaper, and constructed a head on which we placed a poke face. As Dad was 5'11" and quite broad, it was enormous.

Ian parked our trolley outside in readiness to go begging for pennies. However, our mother was adamant that we were not to go and promptly dragged the guy upstairs to her bedroom where she sat it in the Lloyd Loom chair to await its fate.

Later, when Mum was otherwise engaged, Ian hatched a plan. He sent me upstairs, instructing me to throw the guy out of the bedroom window where he would be waiting to catch it. Guiltily I did as I was told and hauled the hideous looking guy onto the window-sill, and pushed it through the window. Unfortunately, at this point, Aunt Cis had gone out the back and was passing beneath the bedroom window as the guy tumbled through the air. She screamed blue murder as it landed on top of her.

Aerial Bombshells were Ian's favourite bangers as they were extremely loud. One year he saved one of these bangers, and duly forgot that he had it. When he made the discovery he was anxious to let it off. It was during the summer when Mr Ruddock who lived next door to Mr Hopper, was painting the front of his house. He was up the top of his ladder when Ian lit the blue touch paper. Ten minutes later an ashen-faced Mr Ruddock was on our doorstep regaling my mother with the details of how he had nearly had a heart attack.

John Shepheard lived next door, and was about five years younger than me. One Guy Fawkes' night Ian accidentally dropped a lighted match onto John's box of fireworks, sending his entire family leaping in all directions to avoid the Catherine Wheels, Rockets and Jumping Jacks.

If I were to list all of Ian's misdemeanours, this book would be the thickness of Tolstoy's *War and Peace* as his antics took place on a daily basis causing us all to live in fear of what was to happen next.

It was decided that he must take after Gran's brother, William Drayton, who was also a prankster and caused mayhem at regular intervals. Like Ian, William Drayton had a mischievous gleam in his eye, and never missed an opportunity to pull off some prank or another.

He and Gran were born and brought up in the little village of Odcombe in Somerset, and due to the severe camber in one of the nearby lanes, he was able to stand outside one of the cottages and with a feather duster tickle the feet of an elderly couple as they lay in bed, because he was parallel with their bedroom window.

Despite it all, Ian was very lovable, and we shared a very happy childhood.

Ian was like our father in that he was very clever with his hands, although not remotely musical. My mother took him to Mrs Biddle for piano lessons, but the pain of listening to him trying to play the *Keel Row* got the better of her, and it was not long before she realised that no amount of tuition was going to improve Ian's ability as a pianist.

However, he could construct anything with his hands, and even made a record player out of his Meccano set. He was fascinated with wires and oil cans, often with disastrous results. Quite how he survived childhood can only be classed as a miracle.

Chapter Two

At a very early age I can remember announcing to my mother that I was going to buy a cow when I grew up. This was received with much mirth and scorn, and I was told that I could not just do that, and that one had to be born into farming. However, being rather a determined child I continued to argue that I would, someday, own a cow and that was that.

The family's only connection with farming was a distant cousin on my mother's side of the family called Rex Drayton. He was Gran's first cousin, and farmed in Montecute, Somerset. We would pay annual visits to his farm in the early 1950s up until the late 1970s when he retired. These visits were the highlights of my life, marred only by the fact that I had to wear a nice dress, with white socks and sandals, and keep quiet, and above all, keep clean. This proved extremely difficult given the conditions in a farmyard, and rather spoilt my enjoyment.

Uncle Rex's wife, Clara, was a superb cook, winning prizes at local shows for her cherry cakes in particular. She made lovely fruit pies which she served with lashings of clotted cream, and as everything was produced on the farm it tasted delicious.

On one occasion, whilst walking around the farm, my father spotted a car in one of the barns. It was plastered in mud, but on closer inspection it turned out to be a brand new Rover. On the back seat was a bale of straw with a broody hen sitting a clutch of eggs. Dad, who would have given his eye teeth for the vehicle, admonished Rex for treating it in such a way. "It's a tool," was Uncle Rex's nonchalant reply.

My grandmother was also into livestock, having had to 'Dig for Victory' during the war, and kept chickens at the bottom of our garden. Before my time, apparently, she had also kept goats for their milk, and together with a large vegetable patch and fruit cage, had kept her family on the fat of the land. My grandfather had made a little cart for the goats that my mother used to drive around in.

I used to love collecting the eggs from the six Rhode Island Reds and six White Wyandottes that lived in a house constructed of asbestos sheeting at the bottom of our garden. They had the run of the garden up until they developed a death wish. It was on a Sunday afternoon whilst Dad was taking a nap, snoring away one minute and risking life and limb trying to avoid the train to Charing Cross the next, as he tried to grab a dozen hens from the line, that seemed bent on committing suicide. Having captured them, a lot of nailing up took place to ensure that it never happened again. They were confined to barracks and had to make do with a wire mesh run, which seemed rather sad as they had been used to better things.

As the hens produced surplus to our requirements, Gran's friend, Rosie Fry, used to have a dozen eggs each week. Rosie read tea leaves, and upon her arrival the kettle would be placed on the gas ring in preparation of her predictions.

Rosie was a short, swarthy looking woman with beady eyes giving her a 'rat-like' appearance. Whilst the tea was brewing there would be a considerable amount of chatter as Rosie updated my Gran on the local scandal. Once the tea and biscuits had been consumed, Rosie would proceed to peer into each cup. Prior to her inspection she would swirl the dregs around, and then place the cup upside down in the saucer thus leaving tea leaves plastered to the sides of the cup.

She would turn the cups this way and that whilst sighing and muttering and looking very puzzled. Predictions of men coming to the house, receiving some news, and the possibility that we might travel somewhere were made. Even at my young age I had grave doubts about Rosie's ability of foretelling the future, and did not believe a word of it, but my mother and grandmother erred on the side of superstition and took it all in.

These weekly prophecies of impending doom, together with predictions of forthcoming good fortune, continued for some years until Rosie became infirm and unable to continue her visits.

My parents had no inclination to keep livestock whatsoever, apart from a cat. Boxer allowed us to live in the house out of the kindness of his heart. He was a beautiful, grey cat, and would lie on our beds and comfort us throughout chicken-pox and measles. He died aged sixteen years, and following a funeral conducted by Ian and me, he was quickly replaced as we could not live without a cat. My grandmother had always been fond of cats and my mother used to tell us stories of how she used to dress their tabby cat up in dolls' clothes and push him around in a pram. Jim was a good tempered, affable cat by all accounts, keeping his teeth to himself and his claws sheathed up; until my mother gave him a toffee! He swore and cursed until my grandmother realised what had happened and managed to free his jaws up.

Pepe was to be Boxer's replacement, and from day one was determined to get the cuckoo out of the clock. He was a highly intelligent cat and planned his attack in great detail. He would sit on the arm of the chair nearest the clock and watch for hours. My mother was adamant that he would one day achieve his aim, but we just laughed, thinking it would be totally impossible as Pepe would have had to know exactly when to jump. As it happened he did know exactly when to jump – twelve noon to be precise. He started to tremble in anticipation as the hands pointed upwards, and then – bingo! The cuckoo, the clock and the cat ended up in a heap on the floor. Most put out at not finding a real bird in the clock, Pepe walked haughtily away leaving the clock in ruins.

My parents were happy to have a cat in the house, but drew the line at keeping a dog. I desperately wanted a dog, but was told that I would have to wait until I had a place of my own. Some years later they were to relent when I broke my arm following a fall from my pony.

My arm was not healing well, and having been plated and then pinned, I was now told that I would require a bone-graft. As I had spent six months incarcerated in plaster, I was not looking forward to remaining in this situation for yet another six months, but, sadly, this was to be the case, and in a moment of pity for me, my parents said I could have a dog.

Mackeson was a Labrador cross. Exactly what he had been crossed with was unknown, but whatever it was must have been big and savage. As his paws were the size of dinner plates, it was agreed that a small basket would be outgrown in no time, so this little, black pup was placed in a basket large enough to accommodate a Great Dane. By morning the basket resembled a pile of chopped firewood. No one was happy at this state of affairs, and it was decided that he would have to sleep on a blanket.

The following morning the first tread of the stairs had been reduced in size, and in its place stood a little heap of wood chippings. No one was happy at this state of affairs either, and Mackie spent his third night in the conservatory. By morning the bottom of the door had all but gone, and long gouge marks graced the side panel.

I tried to explain away his behaviour by saying he was bored, and would settle down once he had completed his course of injections and could be properly exercised.

By the time he received his last injection the house was looking the worse for wear, and Mack and I were most unpopular.

Whilst out on his maiden walk he picked up a piece of discarded tin foil which contained the remnants of food. I bent down and asked him nicely to give it to me. He gave it to me all right, nearly removing three of my fingers. With blood dripping from my hand, I returned home hoping that tetanus would not set in.

This pattern of behaviour was to continue, and it was not long before we were all living in fear of him.

The internal doors of our house had ball catches, making it possible for the dog to go into whichever room he chose. Pushing his shoulder up against the door of the sacrosanct front room, he would make a grand entry as the door slammed against the wall.

23

He would then proceed to recline on the settee. If chastised and commanded to get off, his eyes would glow red and he would bare his teeth. A low growl would put pay to any further attempts at removing him, and we would retreat.

However, a cure was to be found that took the form of a pair of red, rubber gloves. My mother was in the middle of disinfecting the drain that was just outside the back door. At the same time Mackie decided to have a siesta. On seeing him proceeding towards the door of the front room, Aunt Cis gallantly tried to intercept, but Mackie, with his usual air, indicating that when you saw him coming you had best step aside, continued to push past her and make for his chosen destination. Knowing that she was facing defeat, Aunt Cis went out and reported him to my mother who, on receiving this unwelcome news, came in fuming. Complete with red, rubber gloves dripping with disinfectant, she stormed into the front room and confronted the reclining dog. On seeing the gloves, Mack slithered from the settee and keeping a low profile, walked out of the room. My mother stood aghast, hardly believing what she was seeing, and could only assume that she had the gloves to thank.

From that day on we at least had some semblance of control over the animal, but not enough to prevent him from biting us. He would insert his teeth in an arm or leg for no apparent reason, and no member of the family, or visitor to the house, was exempt. Short of kitting ourselves out with red, rubber gloves, and wearing them at all times, there appeared to be nothing we could do.

I was able to take him for walks up until he was almost fully grown, but after that I had problems. My plastered arm was heavy and awkward, and Mackeson was incredibly strong. Malcolm and Ian were commandeered to take him out, which they did under sufferance, but despite being able-bodied, they too struggled to maintain control. We did not feel that it was safe to let him off the lead, fearing that he would eat somebody as he had already nearly killed the dog next door and badly bitten its owner, so long walks had to be undertaken.

Mackie would drag his walker along, flatly refusing to slow

24

down, let alone walk to heel. The only contact he was prepared to have with our heels was with his teeth.

When the walker was on the verge of exhaustion, the only remedy was to quickly loop the end of the lead over a stout fencing post. Alternatively, when approaching a lamp-post, strategically position oneself on one side and, with the dog on the other, frantically wind the lead around the post. Having drawn breath, with legs buckling at the knees, the walker would thankfully return.

One day, following several days of torrential rain, Mackeson asked to go out. As the strongest members of the family were unavailable to take him, Aunt Cis bravely leashed him up and took him out into the garden. Sometime later, my mother, wondering where my aunt had got to, went out only to find Mack dragging Aunt Cis along the ground around the garden. Plastered in mud, and on the verge of tears, she vowed never to take him again.

This sorry state of affairs was to continue for nine months, when he made a big mistake in his choice of victim, and bit Aunt Rene. No one bit Aunt Rene and lived. Mack, therefore, embarked on a one-way trip to the vet's.

A pall of gloom hung over the household for quite some time as, despite his unsociable behaviour, we all missed him and had a certain amount of affection for him. He will certainly never be forgotten. We only have to look at our scars and the memories of him come flooding back.

b

Chapter Three

Whilst quite young I became interested in horses. In those days shop owners and rag and bone men used horses to hawk their wares, and among them was Annie Taylor. Annie had a greengrocer's shop in Crayford. The shop was on the end of a row of three, and a little further down was Farriger's Garage. Annie Taylor owned a big, grey mare that pulled a cart laden with fruit and vegetables. Boxes of apples and oranges, together with whatever else was in season at the time, would be neatly arranged in boxes down one side of the cart, with an assortment of vegetables on the other side. A row of bananas swung from a bar down the middle. Brown paper bags, together with the mare's nosebag, hung on the back, and dangling from beneath was a bucket and a small shovel for collecting up the mare's droppings. We never did know the horse's name, but when we heard the familiar clippety-clop, my brother Ian would shout, "Niggy outside," so as far as we were concerned she was called Niggy.

Niggy would plod along the road, stopping at approximately every sixth house, when she would patiently wait until Annie had finished serving before moving on with Annie walking along behind, her leather money bag swinging from her waist. One day, however, Niggy must have had the Devil in her, for instead of stopping as usual outside our house, she just kept going, breaking into a trot, sending fruit and vegetables in all directions. Poor Annie was demented. She was not terribly athletic, and was struggling to catch up with the horse that by this time was hell bent on getting back to her stable. Annie's shrieks of "Whoa, whoa," fell on deaf ears, and Niggy went even faster. Needless to say, Ian was closely questioned as to whether he had had a hand in the cause of Niggy's uncharacteristic behaviour, but on this occasion it was decided that he was innocent.

The shop next door to Annie's was a grocery cum delicatessen owned by Mr Darney. A large ginger cat used to sit in the window on the bacon slicer and, when the slicer was required, the cat was shooed away only to resume its position when it was available again. I do not think health and safety regulations could have applied in those days, but even if they did Mr Darney never paid much attention, and the customers did not seem to mind a bit of fur with their ham.

Next door to Mr Darney was Mr and Mrs Morrissey's sweet shop.

For some time after the war rationing was still in existence, and we would go along with our coupons with which we could get very little. We would often buy 'hundreds and thousands' as two ounces of these would last several days if carefully eked out. Another favourite were 'bull's-eyes', as these would take forever to suck, and therefore kept us going until the next ration.

Aunt Cis did most of the shopping as she suffered mental health problems making it difficult for her to hold down a job. When my Gran first made the observation that Milbra's behaviour was somewhat different from her other children, she called in Dr Renton, the local GP who was also a close friend. After asking a few hypothetical questions, such as, if Aunt Cis had a little flower, would she water it every day, he proceeded to get her to walk around the dining-room table. Quite how many revolutions of the table Aunt Cis made before Dr Renton decided that she was, indeed, a bit odd, I know not, and quite how this procedure assisted him in making a diagnosis remains a mystery. My Gran was left wondering who was the most odd out of the two of them.

Aunt Cis had worked for a baker soon after leaving school, but after about a week the baker told my Gran that she would have to go as she talked incessantly, and he did not know whether he was making doughnuts or meringues. However, she was an invaluable help to my mother and grandmother as she would keep the house clean and tidy, polishing the furniture and floors until they gleamed, and scraping the fly droppings from the mirror with her thumb nail before cleaning it with Windolene. She spent a lot of time looking after my brothers and me, and was one of the kindest and most unselfish people one could meet. Nothing was ever too much trouble for her, and she would go out to the shops in all weathers if something was urgently needed.

She was also prone to being on the receiving end of Ian's pranks.

Situated against one wall in the dining-room was a long, oblong box which we called the 'coffer box'. Ian and I would often sit on this box, sucking our bull's-eyes, and Aunt Cis would join us. She listened to us chattering, and would sing and read to us.

One day, whilst Ian and I were sat on the coffer box, he said that he was going to call Aunt Cis in to sit with us, and that when she was about to sit down, I was to stand up. In came Aunt Cis, and walked towards the box. She turned around to sit down. At the same time Ian and I stood up. Ian lifted the lid of the box, and Aunt Cis disappeared leaving only the soles of her feet sticking up.

Aunt Cis was rather an outspoken person with a keen sense of humour which occasionally got her into hot water.

One day, having paid a visit to the sweet shop, Mrs Morrissey accused her of having 'designs' on her husband, Gus. What with Aunt Cis's flat feet and matching chest and Gus Morrissey with his beer gut and bald head, they were not exactly Romeo and Juliet, so quite where Mrs Morrissey got her ideas from is a mystery. However, Aunt Cis soon put a stop to Mrs Morrissey's fantasies by telling her that she would not want Gussie soused.

Mrs Wenderot, together with her husband Henry and daughter Stella, owned a paper shop along the Dartford Road. Henry was a very tall man with a bear-like appearance, and walked with a pronounced limp, causing him to lurch rather than stride. I used to find this very disconcerting when he was walking towards me, and I would feel really quite frightened. One day Aunt Cis returned from the paper shop and announced that Henry had died. A bit later on that week, Mrs Wenderot showed Aunt Cis some photographs of Henry laid out in his coffin, to which she said that it was the best she had seen him look.

I used to be fascinated by people when I was a child, and would take in every detail of someone's appearance and mannerisms.

Daphne Lockyer owned the Post Office along the Dartford Road, and lived over the shop. She was very slow at her job, giving me ample time to study her. It was not unusual to have to queue for at least fifteen minutes to be served, even when there were hardly any customers in the shop. When counting out the pound notes she would stroke and stretch them. My father pointed out to her one day that no matter how much she tried to stretch them they would not go any further. He received a look that could have killed.

Daphne had a minor bird that lived in a cage in the shop, dangling beneath a shelf that was stacked high with packs of wool. She would keep up a constant conversation with the bird saying, "Oou, Oou," and the bird would reply, "Oou, Oou." After a while it was enough to drive you mad, but you had to put up with it until at last you had been served and could escape.

Miss Harber was another character that came under my scrutiny. May owned a little sweet shop along the Dartford Road. It was actually the front room of her house, and many a visit was paid to May on our way home from West Hill School.

She was quite an austere person, standing no nonsense from us children. "Do you want a Lucky Dip or not?" she would demand in a vexed tone of voice. If we did it meant May having to walk around the counter and through a gate as she had to remove the lid from the enormous water butt in which the Lucky Dips were kept. May was of rather large proportions, making this manoeuvre through the little gate quite an effort. If we changed our minds after she had prised herself through the gap, we would be thrown out of the shop.

I must admit that we did use to play May up a bit. The big jars of sweets were lined up on the shelves behind the counter. As the pear-drops were on the top shelf a step ladder was required to get them down. One by one we would all ask for pear-drops. Having served the first one of us, she would return the jar to its rightful place, only to have to go up the ladder again to serve the next one of us. May was so methodical that she would never have dreamed of leaving the jar on the counter until we had all been served, so she provided us with much entertainment as she swayed about on the little ladder. The game would be given away when one of us was unable to stifle a giggle, and again we would be heaved out of the shop clutching pear-drops that we did not really want but had to have if we wanted to watch May performing with the ladder.

Chapter Four

When a friend of mine became pregnant, and could no longer keep her pony, she asked if I would like to have him. Needless to say I was overjoyed, as I had been riding for some considerable time and had dreamed of owning my own pony one day. Persuading my parents was an uphill task, but finally they agreed, and I was on cloud nine.

Billy was a bay cob standing 14.2 hands high. He had a white star on his forehead and a white sock on each back foot. Aged fourteen, by this time he knew his way about, and could go lame to order if he thought a horse show was imminent. We had a great deal of fun together, and he taught me a lot.

The pony had a hogged mane. For the uninitiated this means that he had not got one. The back of his neck resembled a brush as the hair was clipped off at the roots. The style suited him being as he was a cob, but, unfortunately, unlike his previous owner, I did not possess a pair of clippers, and it was not long before Billy looked as if he had had a nasty fright with his hair standing up about four inches from his neck. Being as he had always been hogged, it would not willingly lay over and looked a terrible sight.

Dad owned a pair of hair clippers that I believe he had inherited from his father. These were kept in a sturdy, cardboard box, wrapped carefully in a piece of cloth, in the second drawer down on the right-hand side of the dressing-table in my parent's bedroom.

On seeing the dreadful state of Billy's mane, my mother asked me what I intended to do about it. I explained that there was nothing I could do without a pair of clippers. She aided and abetted me in borrowing Dad's, but told me to say nothing about it and be sure to thoroughly clean them before returning them to their rightful place in the dressing-table drawer.

I wasted no time, and before long the pony's hairstyle was restored to normal. Horsehair and grease was carefully removed, and the clippers returned looking none the worse for providing Billy with a Mohican.

A couple of weeks later my father noticed that Ian's hair was beginning to look a little untidy around the edges. My mother had been putting off taking him to the hairdresser, but assured Dad that she would take him the following week. As it was a Sunday when Dad made the observation that Ian needed a haircut, nothing could be done by a professional barber, so Dad decided to get the clippers out. Mum and I stared at each other in horror. Mum frantically tried to dissuade Dad from carrying out his intentions, protesting that Ian had a 'cow's lick', and needed the attention of a qualified barber.

Dad was having none of it, and went upstairs for the clippers. He took out a little can of sewing machine oil and proceeded to squeeze the handles of the clippers in order to work it in. Dead silence reigned whilst this was being done, with Mum and me hoping and praying that the oil would somehow recondition them. Ian was sat on a dining chair over by the window, and a 'flowery' apron belonging to Aunt Cis draped around his shoulders. Sadly for Ian the oil had no effect, and he screamed the place down as the hairs from the back of his neck were viciously pulled out one by one. Blissfully unaware that his prized clippers had been used on a horse, Dad, unsympathetically, told Ian to be quiet, and keep his head still.

Finally, to spare Ian any more agony, my mother confessed that the clippers had been used to hog Billy, and I spent the rest of the day confined to my bedroom with Ian standing outside the door, rubbing the back of his neck and threatening never to speak to me again.

My father was adamant that he was having nothing whatsoever to do with the pony and that I would have to earn the money required to pay for his keep. However, he did become involved when I fell off, badly breaking my arm in three places, and was in hospital for some time. It was an easy task during the summer months as it was just a case of checking that he had a leg at each corner on a daily basis, but during the winter months he was stabled at night, thus creating the tasks of mucking him out, making his bed and feeding him.

One of the ponies with which he shared his field was a pony called Sweep. Sweep was totally neglected by his owner, a Miss Mackintosh. She would visit him infrequently, but when she did put in an appearance he was overjoyed to see her. The rest of the time he was positively lethal. He would charge towards me, and on one occasion managed to knock me to the ground and bite a chunk out of my shoulder.

Dad was duly warned of Sweep's vicious nature, and told to be sure to fasten the gate securely when entering the field lest Sweep should escape, as getting out was Sweep's sole aim in life. Unfortunately, Dad had every faith in Sweep and did not secure the gate. My mother was in attendance, but refused point blank to enter the field as she was by no means a 'horsey' person. She was convinced that one end bit, the other end kicked, and wanted nothing to do with the bit in the middle. When she saw Sweep worrying at the chain loosely wrapped around the gate-post, she promptly took to her heels and fled. Dad was out of sight in the stable tending to Billy quite unaware of the drama that was unfolding outside. On his return, the gate was ajar, with no sign of Sweep or my mother. He ran up the road and found Sweep grazing on the verge. A chase ensued up and down the road, Dad determined to get Sweep returned to the field, and Sweep equally determined to evade capture. At last he was free, and he intended to stay that way.

Dad got more and more exasperated, and took hold of a stick having reached the conclusion that he was going to have to get physical with the beast – I think he said beast – it began with a 'b' anyway. Sweep saw the stick and decided that he too, would have to change tactics, so he approached father, swung round, and lashed out with both hind legs, 'like pistons' as my father was to describe later, and on many other occasions when recalling the incident.

Dad, absolutely fuming by now, kicked out at Sweep's backside, thus incurring a double inguinal hernia. At the ferocity of Dad's attack, Sweep realised the game was up, and returned to the field.

With me now out of hospital, and Dad now in hospital to have his hernia repaired, things returned to normal, and I resumed my chores in order to fund Billy's keep by running errands for various elderly people, and picking groundsel for a neighbour's hamster or whatever it was.

Nellie Apps was a large contributor to my pony fund, as I used to run errands and do little jobs for her accompanied by Ian. Being as there was only eighteen months difference in our ages, we tended to do everything together and were practically joined at the hip.

Nellie was a dear old lady, and a neighbour of Aunt Rene and Uncle Will. She was always so grateful for all we did for her, and on arrival would ask, "Would you like a sweetie, dear?" She would go over to an old, oak chest of drawers, and take out a little bag of toffees. This was done very slowly as she had arthritis in her hands, and we used to think that we would never get the sweet that day.

Three items in Nellie's house used to fascinate me. One was the big, old oak chest of drawers where the sweets were kept, as it was heavily carved and looked beautiful. Another was a pair of bellows propped up beside the fireplace, and last of all was the big grandfather clock which had a sinister tick. I felt as though it was watching me, and always stood in awe of it.

Nellie loved the birds, and each day would put bread to soak in a little bowl for them. She said it was bad for them if it was not soaked first, and when it was soggy, she would squeeze out the excess water and we would throw it up onto the roof of her shed. Unfortunately for the birds, Nellie's next door neighbour owned a cat with which Nellie would wage war on a daily basis. She would talk to the cat in her thin, reedy voice saying, "You're a nice pussy, but you will not leave the birds alone, leave them alone." It made not one iota of difference, and the cat would remain strategically positioned beside the shed ready for the kill.

Once Nellie's jobs were done, Ian and I would go to Aunt Rene's.

All the houses in the terrace were on three floors. The little cosy living-room and large kitchen were on the ground floor. As the ground floor was below the height of the road, it was quite dark in these two rooms, with only a small window in the kitchen, and a slightly larger one in the living-room.

A heavy, iron mangle stood just below the window in the kitchen, where Ian and I would labour hard and long mangling washing, and would be rewarded with a little bowl of icing sugar and coconut each, plus a donation for Billy. If we forgot to empty the bowl of water that we had wrung out of the washing before it ran over, we were rewarded with a good telling off.

We loved the tiny living-room. A gas mantle provided the lighting, and we would often be sent down to May Harber's to buy a new mantle as they were very brittle, and would suddenly 'pop' leaving the room in darkness.

It was like a snug with two arm chairs, one either side of the open fireplace. A sideboard was in an alcove beneath the staircase on which the mantle clock sat between two silver bowls. One day I made a grave mistake and mentioned to Aunt Rene that I liked her gold bowls. Snorting with indignation, she made a dive for a cupboard from where she emerged clutching a can of Silvo and a piece of rag. Measuring out a small quantity of the thick, white fluid onto the rag, she began vigorously rubbing the side of one of the bowls as if trying to conjure up a genie, whilst admonishing me for being so rude! Apart from a small, drop-leaf table pushed up against the staircase wall, there was no room for anything else. In summer it was pleasantly cool, and lovely and warm in winter.

A sitting-room and a small bedroom were on the second floor. Aunt Grace, Uncle Will's eldest sister, occupied this small bedroom on her occasional visits.

I greatly admired Aunt Grace. She entered a career in nursing on leaving school, and at the young age of eighteen had to have a breast removed due to cancer. Three years later the disease was discovered in her other breast, and this also was removed.

Despite this tragedy, she was a lovely person and always full of fun. She had no children of her own and made up for it by spoiling Ian and I.

When she was nursing at St. Nicholas' Hospital in Plumstead, an elderly patient who was totally blind gave her a doll that she had made. This doll was truly amazing. It was approximately one foot long, and was two dolls in one. The first doll was a white lady who I called 'My Lady'. She wore a beautiful dress made of white, silky material and black lace. Leg o'mutton sleeves were trimmed with black velvet and red felt covered her hands. A string of pearls was fastened around her neck. Red braid bows were tied around the sleeves and waistline. When this doll was inverted, instead of legs under the skirt as one would expect, there was the head of a lovely black doll on the other side. She wore a red turban and a check patterned dress also with leg o'mutton sleeves made from mauve, silk material. The cuffs were made of black velvet, and trimmed with white lace. An apron was tied around her waist, and she had blue and white beads with matching earrings.

One day, when Aunt Grace was visiting, she asked me to go up to the little bedroom with her where she produced this incredible doll from between layers of tissue paper. She told me that she wanted me to have it as she was confident that I would take great care of it. Being a bit of a tom-boy, I was not terribly enthusiastic about playing with dolls, but I was overjoyed at being given this very special doll, which to this day is still wrapped in the original tissue paper in which it was presented to me, and provides me with very happy memories of my dear Aunt Grace.

Having nursed throughout her life in general hospitals, her last appointment was in a hospital for retired naval personnel located in Gillingham, Kent.

Ian and I would often accompany Aunt Rene and Uncle Will on visits to this hospital where Aunt Grace was Matron.

A lift provided easy access to all the floors for the elderly residents, except when Ian and I arrived on the scene. On these occasions, just as they would enter the lift to ascend, we would press the appropriate button to bring them down again. Once back to where they had started, we would send them up again. This would continue until Aunt Rene came in search of us, having presumably had a premonition that Ian might be partaking of some prank or another. Prior to her intervention, the old Commodores would be going up and down like yo-yos. Looking the picture of innocence, we would follow Aunt Rene back to Aunt Grace's study where we would be supplied with soft drinks and fresh cream cakes that we most definitely did not deserve. A good hiding would have been more appropriate.

The third bedroom in Aunt Rene and Uncle Will's house was unused save for a dart board hanging on the wall where Ian and I had many tournaments and arguments.

The sitting-room was quite large, and contained Uncle Will's gramophone which we were allowed to play. This was a contraption that had a handle to wind it up, and a very heavy 'arm' containing a tungsten needle. We were only allowed to play three records, these being Sir Roger de Coverley, In The Mood, and White Horse Inn. As these records had been played many times, the quality was poor, and had we accidentally broken them our Aunt and Uncle would not have been terribly upset. All the decent records were kept well out of our reach so it was as well that we liked the three that we had access to. However, on one occasion, by balancing precariously on the arm of a chair, Ian managed to get hold of Three Coins In A Fountain. Quietly closing the sitting-room door so that it would not be heard by Aunt Rene downstairs, he put it on the turntable. Unfortunately, he managed to jog the needle causing it to damage the record so that it went Three Coins In A F f f f f f f f f f f f.

Thankfully, this had not been one of Aunt Rene or Uncle Will's favourites, so Ian was spared a clip round the ear, unlike the time when he bent the hammers of the mantle clock causing it to sound like the arrival of Mr Whippy.

When Aunt Rene reached the point at which she could no

longer stand the sound of Sir Roger de Coverley coupled with the constant tap tap tapping of the darts, we would be sent home.

Judy was Aunt Rene and Uncle Will's dog. She was a mongrel, black, white and tan, and quite a large animal. Taking her for walks boosted my pony fund, and was one of my favourite jobs. Dudsbury Road was an unmade up road that ran beside Aunt Rene's house, so Ian and I did not have too far to go on wet days. Judy was thoroughly spoilt, and every Friday night she was given a bar of Five Boys. This was a very thin chocolate bar with a picture of five boys on the wrapper, their hair plastered down with Brylcreem. Judy would growl if she thought Ian or I were going to eat a bit of it, and would bare her teeth, but she never harmed us despite her threats. Needless to say Ian would pretend to eat a piece just to wind her up.

When our Aunt and Uncle went on holiday, Judy came to stay with us. We were sorry when they returned as we missed Judy terribly when she had to go back, but Mum was glad to see the back of the dog's hairs on the carpets.

Uncle Will was a keen gardener and grew all the vegetables required for him and Aunt Rene, plus surplus for Nellie and other neighbours. A huge Victoria plum tree graced the bottom of the garden, which would be laden with fruit every year. Aunt Rene always insisted that we wash the plums, cut them in half and check for maggots. This always seemed an unnecessary chore to me as I was impatient to sink my teeth into the delicious fruit. That was until one day I found a maggot!

Uncle Will had fought in the war, being posted all over the place. Numerous photographs of him were in the family album, including one of him together with other troops standing in front of the pyramids. We always regarded him as a hero and had a great respect for him. Fortunately he came home in one piece, apart from a lump of shrapnel in an index finger.

He had a shove-ha'penny board with which he and Aunt Rene played on dark winter nights, interspersed with games of dominoes. Percy Batten used to be invited round for a weekly session of dominoes. Percy lived next door and was a dear old chap, if not a bit eccentric. He did not have wallpaper on any of the walls in the house, with the exception of the first flight of stairs which he papered with the front covers of the John Bull magazine. His house always seemed much darker than Aunt Rene's, and smelt very musty. His hair was as black as a raven's, even when he reached the grand old age of ninety, a phenomenon which he attributed to a daily application of methylated spirit, making Percy highly inflammable, but looking younger than his years.

Chapter Five

As Dad had made it abundantly clear that he had no intention of paying anything towards Billy's keep, I was really pleased when a man turned up with three horses to share the grazing in the field. They comprised of Panda, a piebald cob standing about 15 hands, Thunder, a skewbald, slightly lighter in build, and a chestnut pony.

Patrick seemed a nice enough chap, albeit a wide boy. He was in his mid thirties, married with several children. Shortly after his arrival he asked me if I would look after his horses as he thought he might be going away. He said he would know the following day if he would definitely be going, but he was not sure how long he would be gone; it could be six months. I thought it all a bit odd, but thrilled that I could have the use of his horses to earn money by giving rides.

The following day came and went with no sign of Patrick who did 'go away' for six months to Maidstone Prison.

I built up quite a clientele for riding lessons and made enough money to keep Billy in the lap of luxury, plus a few shillings for myself.

When Patrick had done his time, he returned looking pale and thin but in good spirits. He was pleased to see that his horses had been well cared for, and gave me permission to continue to use them as much as I liked. He continued to 'go away' for various periods of time, but was always cheerful. I never did know if he knew my name as he always called me gal, but, there again, I may not have known his real name either.

Another great help to me was Harry Rowlestone. Harry was quite elderly, short, bent and wizened. He always had a piece of mauve clover clasped in the corner of his mouth which gave the impression that either a moth had landed on him or he had a very nasty sore. Either way, it was not a pretty sight.

Harry used to farm on quite a large scale in days gone by, but now only kept two house cows and two shire horses. If I happened to be around at milking time, Harry would let me have a go. Milking is an art, make no mistake. Get it wrong and you have a very annoyed cow, and warm, wet clothing. Many a time have I squirted the milk up my sleeve and had the cow empty the contents of the bucket over my feet in exasperation. This would be when Harry would intervene as he saw the milk for his tea and cornflakes disappearing. His gnarled fingers would make short work of the job, with all the milk safely deposited in the bucket and a happy, contented cow quietly eating her cake.

The word 'stress' did not feature in Harry's vocabulary. Everything was done in a quiet, methodical way, with a place for everything, and everything in its place. His animals always seemed willing to co-operate with him, with no need for the use of a dog or stick, although he did own a lurcher called Jip. When Jip died, he got another lurcher and called that Jip. It transpired that all the dogs he had owned over the years had been given the same name. The cows knew the time that Harry would arrive to milk them and would be standing ready to be milked at the door to the shippen, and Peter, the shire horse that he mainly used, would go to him immediately he was called. There was never any hassle and it all looked so easy.

Despite his small stature, Harry was incredibly strong and would lift heavy milk churns and such like with ease. How he managed to tack Peter up without the use of a step-ladder I do not know, as Peter was 18 hands and Harry had shrunk over the years to five foot nothing.

Looking around at the pace of life today and the stress that accompanies it, makes me realise that Harry had it right. He made quite an impact on me and made me even more determined to pursue my dream of owning a smallholding someday.

Once a week Harry would drive Peter down to the dog racing track in Crayford to collect straw that had been used to bed down the greyhounds. This he would bring home and give some to me for Billy's winter bedding, and keep a supply for his two horses. In addition, he used to bring home the remains of the boiled bullocks' heads that had been used to feed the greyhounds. As a consequence, I did not have to buy straw, but had to wage a constant battle with rats. The straw was a godsend, but the rats were a menace. Harry used to put the sacks of bones on old carts that were littered around the field. In summer they would stink to high heaven. From time to time the rats would move house, and armies of them could be seen making for a different cart. There would be a thick, black, solid line of them. The sacks would rock on the carts as they climbed out. I used to feel a mixture of fascination and horror at the sight, but I was never frightened of them. I would not dare mention the rats at home as my mother would have had me, Harry, rats and all fumigated, so it was a well kept secret. As were my jaunts to the dog track with Harry to get the straw, as my mother most definitely would not have approved of me going. Harry used to let me take the reins and drive Peter on the way back which was the highlight of the trip for me.

Jumbo was Harry's other horse, but unlike Peter, had a nasty nature and would bite. He was given a wide berth unless, for some reason, Harry was using him to pull the cart, and then my friends and I would climb on board the cart feeling secure in the knowledge that Jumbo was anchored down by leather straps and chains, and we were over sixteen feet from his mouth.

One day Harry had used Jumbo for a trip to the Crayford Greyhound Stadium to collect the straw and bones instead of Peter. As he was proposing to use Jumbo again a little later on, he left the horse harnessed to the cart standing in the field. The reins were knotted over the top of his back, leaving him free to roam, albeit with the burden of the cart in tow.

Unable to resist the temptation to climb aboard, my friends and I sat ourselves down in the bottom of the cart where we chatted and laughed. Suddenly, Jumbo ceased grazing and started to make his way across the field. He broke into a trot and before long was going hell for leather with the cart bouncing along behind, often up on two wheels. There was nothing we could do apart from cling to the sides of the cart for grim death. Jumbo was going flat out and it seemed the cart would turn over at any minute. Fortunately before serious injury was incurred he came to a halt. Severely battered and bruised, we quickly made our exit.

My bedroom window overlooked the field and, one night shortly after this incident, I heard a shot coming from that direction. We were never to see Jumbo again.

Before I managed to get a stable built in the field, I rented a stable from Harry for two shillings and sixpence a month situated approximately half a mile from the field. It was an old shippen with individual stalls for cows with built-in granite mangers, and channels and drains in the floor. Rusty iron rings were attached to the cobweb bedecked walls, and birds' nests snuggled between the woodworm riddled beams in the roof. Overall it was a tranquil scene, and I could not help feeling totally relaxed when listening to Billy munching away on his hay in the half-light.

The stable was about half a mile from our house but seemed like ten miles in the winter. Kent can be very cold with a considerable amount of snow in the winter months which would make the going particularly hard.

During the winter of 1962/63 Billy was stabled night and day as the thickness of the snow made the roads to the field impassable. The water trough froze solid, so water had to be carried from home. Several journeys had to be made as I only had one pair of hands, and Billy had an enormous thirst. I would trudge back and forth with my buckets in the morning before school, only to have to repeat the performance at the other end of the day. If I had the misfortune to slip and fall over, it would take twice as long. This particular winter was exceptionally bad, but normally we had only moderate snowfalls, and I would ride him down to the field which was about half a mile from the stable.

When the snow was very thick, his hooves would become clogged solid and by the time we reached the field it was as though he was on rockers. I used to try chipping away at it before taking him back to his stable in the evening, but it was to no avail as my hoof pick was no match for the ice. In the morning I would find four lumps of ice buried in the straw.

I was doggedly devoted to Billy and would do anything for him. My family thought me mad turning out in all weathers when I could have been by the fire, but I was happy to do it and really appreciated my home and the warmth when I got in.

Aunt Rene and Uncle Will used to spend Christmas with us, arriving on Christmas Eve, and returning home on Boxing Night. My uncle used to enjoy accompanying me on my jaunts to wait on Billy, and on our return from stable duties we would stop at houses and sing carols.

Another pleasure I derived from my walks to the stable was looking at the skyscapes in the early morning, particularly in the winter when it would be a mixture of ice-blue, pink, gold and grey. It was certainly worth getting up for.

On days when I would be competing at a gymkhana, I used to take Billy home in order to bath him. A right-of-way ran around the back of the terrace of houses and I would have to lead him along, through a little wooden gate and over a manhole cover. Our neighbours were all very nice and raised no objections.

In addition to the other horses that I have already mentioned, Billy shared his field with Sonny, a 16.2 hands high chestnut gelding. He was owned by a very posh looking lady who spoke with a Cockney accent. She always wore full riding habit and looked very regal, that was up until she opened her mouth. Sonny was always immaculately turned out, and between them they looked quite outstanding.

She was married with two children, and on the days that she competed at horse shows her mother, who, like my own mother, had no interest in horses whatsoever, would tag along with the children in tow, and her daughter's husband would be left at home with a packet of fish fingers for his lunch.

On one occasion, I had hacked from Crayford to Southfleet to a show, and on arrival Billy wanted to have a roll as was his custom if he had hacked a considerable distance. Whilst I was removing his saddle I noticed this lady's mum standing close by with the children. As Billy got down onto his knees she turned towards him and witnessed him flopping over onto his side. "Christ," she gasped, " 'ee's fainted."

Southfleet Show was always my favourite. People would travel from miles around to attend, and the box-park would contain everything from dilapidated Land-Rovers towing trailers held together with baler cord and good will, to turbo-charged, six-wheeled, six-horse gin palaces.

One would also see every possible combination of horse and rider. There would be tall, gangly teenagers still riding their first ponies, who, if they had chosen to, could have fitted wheels to their boots and used them as stabilisers. Then there would be the petite little girl with 17hh-plus of seething malevolence beneath her, who would rather be anywhere other than at a horse show, but her parents were full of enthusiasm and wished to fulfil their dreams through their poor, hapless daughter.

In the warm-up area one would often hear colourful and unladylike language with its roots firmly embedded in the Anglo-Saxon as young ladies tried to kick their disinterested horses into life.

One family that I remember well had twelve children. The older ones would career around on Thelwell type ponies whilst the younger children trailed along behind the push-chair that contained the youngest member of the family. On this particular occasion a horse had broken loose and was causing mayhem, sending spectators scattering in all directions. The horse managed to make contact with the push-chair thus throwing the child out. Gasps were heard from people who had witnessed the event, and the child was retrieved, fortunately uninjured. The father then ambled across and, on seeing that the child was his, casually remarked, "It's all right, it's only one of ours."

All in all, it was a good day out.

45

On our return from the shows, Billy would once again trundle around the right-of-way, past Tom and Jim Brown's house and Dave and Joan Shepheard's for a rub down and an apple before being returned to his field.

Chapter Six

Tom and Jim were brothers and had lived at the end of the terrace for many years with their parents. When the parents died, Tom and Jim remained. Tom was stone deaf and as a result had never worked. He stayed at home doing household chores whilst Jim went out to work.

Between preparing meals for Jim and himself, Tom did little else but sit in a big, wooden captain's chair, the side of his outstretched index fingers resting on the arms giving the impression that he had flippers rather than hands. He always wore a brown suit complete with a waistcoat irrespective of the time of year. His stout boots were black and the long laces would be wound around his ankles before being tied in a knot.

Pennies were kept in an assortment of little tins, mainly ones that had contained lozenges at one time, and Ian and I were sent round to Tom on a regular basis with a sixpenny piece to ask him for six pennies as our bus fare to school was one penny. We would catch the trolley bus to school in the morning, walk home for lunch, bus back, then walk home again, thus costing four pence a day between us, so Tom's never ending supply of pennies was a godsend to my mother. It used to seem quite an effort on Tom's part to get out of the chair in order to go to the cupboard where the tins were kept as he seemed very stiff, and we would become agitated if we had cut it a bit fine in going round in case we were late for school, particularly if he asked us a question, and we somehow had to make him understand what we were saying without the aid of pencil and paper.

When war broke out, Jim was conscripted, leaving Tom alone in the house. My family, together with our next door neighbours, Dave and Joan, kept an eye on Tom, getting him out of the house when the sirens went off alerting them to an air-raid, and taking round meat pies and milk puddings, plus any other items of food that they thought he would enjoy.

Poor Tom had obviously heard of neither dentist or toothbrush, and the few teeth he had were encrusted in a shell of plaque which, together with his profound deafness, caused him to pronounce 'S' as 'SH'. "Allo, push," he would say to our cat, " 'Ave you cawd a moush?" whilst stroking him so vigorously the cat was nearly flattened to the ground. Conversation between our cat and Tom was quite straightforward. However, the same could not be said when we tried to converse, due to Tom's total lack of hearing. Notes were written on any scraps of paper that happened to be to hand at the time and put in front of Tom's face.

When Jim was posted abroad during the war, Tom could not understand why no one could tell him exactly where Jim was. Having nearly reached screaming pitch, having written copious notes trying to explain that it was not possible to tell him where Jim was, in desperation my mother suggested that he go over the road and ask Vic Sutton. Vic was always tinkering with some mechanical appliance or another, and when he had finished invariably it never worked again. When Tom came back he announced, "Itch no yush arshkin' Vic, 'ee'sh 'arf bludgy gormlish." My mother probably felt like writing a note of agreement.

Tom nearly came to a sticky end due to his lack of hearing. One night the sirens went off, but the air-raid had already commenced and there was insufficient time to get Tom out and down to the shelter at the bottom of the garden. When the all clear sounded, my parents rushed round to Tom. They found him in bed, fully clothed, boots and all, covered in soot from the chimney and plaster from the ceiling, with only the whites of his eyes showing. "I thawd I feld a bid of a jar," he said. It transpired

48

Gran's family: Minnie, Irene, Nancy, Gran, Edward and Milbra.

My father, mother and grandmother.

My father on his Francis Barnett with myself, Ian and Malcolm.

Odcombe Church, where my grandmother worshipped as a child.

Ian and me.

Uncle Rex with his dog and Gipsy.

Aunt Cis.

Pepe the clock wrecker!

Billy with
his mane
hogged.

Billy before his
haircut with
Dad's cherished
clippers!

The
dreaded
Sweep.

My dear Aunt Grace.

Aunt Grace's doll – My Lady.

The same doll inverted.

Uncle Will second from left in front of the Pyramids in Egypt.

My Wedding Day.

The intrepid Miss Bannister.

Chris receiving his cup for the best flower display.

that the houses directly opposite had been completely demolished, and various walls and doors of the houses that had been left standing had changed places. But Tom, bless him, had only felt a bit of a jar.

Malcolm vividly recalls another occasion when the sirens again sounded too late for people to reach shelter. He was playing in the garden when the siren went off, and as instructed, went straight down into the shelter. However, as he was not joined by the other family members, went up the garden to the house. Inside was utter chaos.

Prior to the effect of the blast, my mother had been winding skeins of wool into balls with the help of Aunt Cis who sat as if being crucified whilst holding out the skeins, Gran had been busy in the kitchen and Aunt Rene was sitting on the toilet. Mum now had all the wool tightly wound around her neck, nearly choking her, Gran was trapped behind a wall that in better times had divided the dining-room from the front room, and Aunt Rene was still sitting on the toilet, but the door had blown off its hinges and was lying in splinters at the foot of the stairs, whilst the front door had been blown up the stairs leaving poor Aunt Rene well and truly caught with her drawers down.

Joan and Dave Shepheard next door had suffered a similar fate. Joan's parents, Mr and Mrs Dudney, lived with them, and following this episode the Reverend Henry Hebden Hurwood from St. Paulinus Church, Crayford, paid them a visit. The vicar was not known to worry too much about the welfare of his flock, and no one saw hair nor hide of him unless they attended his church services. Mr Dudney answered what was left of the front door. Registering his surprise at seeing the Rev. Hurwood he commented that it was a pity that despite having lived there for over twenty-five years it had taken a German bomb to get a visit from the vicar. Mr Dudney's actual words are unprintable as he was not overly enamoured with the vicar at the best of times, and whilst he was standing in a pile of rubble that had once been his home, proved to be a bad time for the Reverend to choose to call. Thus ended any pastoral care that Mr Dudney had been about to receive.

Having got through the war physically unscathed, Tom's brother Jim returned and things resumed there usual routine. Jim went off to work but seemed a bit strange. The war had obviously taken its toll on him mentally, and when Tom was admitted to hospital due to increasing immobility due to arthritis, Jim became very withdrawn. My brothers and I loved Tom, but had always been wary of Jim, and delivered the food parcels to him under duress.

Tragedy was to strike shortly after Tom's departure. One evening there was a knock on our front door. It was our neighbour, Joan Shepheard, who announced that Jim had 'done something to himself'. Thinking that perhaps Jim had badly cut himself or something to that effect, my father, along with Malcolm, went round to see what they could do to help. The fact that Joan's hair was practically standing on end, and her face was ghostly white, should have indicated that it was somewhat more than a minor injury.

In those days houses had gas mantles for lighting, and although most houses had been converted over to electricity, some people retained their gas mantles. Tom and Jim still lit theirs, and this was to add to the horror that was about to unfold.

Tom and Jim never used their front door; therefore, we always went in through the back door that was never locked, night or day. A solitary gas mantle was kept lit in the hallway, and this provided the only source of light. It flickered in the draught, and cast a blue/grey shadow everywhere, thus creating a very spooky atmosphere which used to really frighten Ian and me when delivering the pies and puddings during the dark winter months. All would be dark, silent and eerie, and so it was on this particular night.

My father and brother went in through the back door which led straight into the kitchen. On the table was a plate of food that Joan had minutes before taken in for Jim's supper. All was silent, so they called out to Jim, and on receiving no answer, walked on into the hallway which led to the foot of the stairs. Due to the back door being open, the draught was causing the gas mantle to flicker, casting shadows up the stairs, and in so doing increased

50

the tension that was building. Malcolm decided to go upstairs as Jim was obviously not in either the front or back room, and he thought he may be in the bathroom. Malcolm was never to forget this moment. Jim had rigged up a clothes-line in the loft, and was now dangling over the stairs by his neck, illuminated in a blue/grey haze.

The police were called and unceremoniously cut the rope, and dragged Jim down the stairs. Malcolm was horrified at the sound of the body bumping down each stair, to say nothing of Jim's appearance having been swinging from the beams for some considerable time. My father, on the other hand, seemed quite unfazed having worked in a lunatic asylum for many years.

Jim was bundled into a makeshift coffin and taken away.

Whenever there was a drama of any description in our house, Aunt Cis was sent down to the off-licence at the bottom of our road. On this occasion a large bottle of brandy was purchased and was consumed into the small hours as we were all too scared to go to bed. Malcolm insisted on giving Ian and I an account of Jim's face in graphic detail making sleep almost impossible for at least a week. Joan came in and partook of the brandy, and gave her version of events. At the conclusion of our 'inquest' it was agreed that Jim had never really got over his experiences in the war as he had not seemed quite the same on his return, and when Tom was taken into hospital, he became depressed. Joan remembered seeing him buying the clothes-line in the hardware shop in Crayford about a week prior to pegging himself out on it, so it was clearly premeditated.

As there was now no one to look after Tom he remained in hospital and was later transferred into a home. He was very happy there as he was well cared for and appeared to be a favourite with all the staff. One member of staff took him to the seaside for the day in her car. Tom had never seen the sea in his life and had never been in a car. He told my mother that he had thoroughly enjoyed the trip, but did not think much of the car as he could not stand up in it.

*   *   *   *

51

At this point I feel I must include the 'Tale of Bunny Morris'. Bunny was a friend of Malcolm's, and sang in my brother's choir, having a fine tenor voice. He was rather an effete young man who was studying for the ministry in order to follow in the footsteps of his father who was an Anglican Vicar.

Bunny had a 'Mummy' whose life's work was to ensure that Bunny was coddled and cared for. This care was extreme in the highest degree. His hair was brushed and his shoes were polished by Mummy, he was always wrapped up in his little 'cardy' and he was exhorted at all times to be a good boy, and he duly obliged.

This was in the days of National Service, and Bunny, his studies completed, received one truly awful morning, a bulky, brown envelope which contained an invitation from the Queen requesting his presence at an establishment which gave medical examinations to young men that they considered fit to accept the Queen's shilling.

Unable to impress the Army of his impending death from having dropped arches, Bunny was requested to board a train bound for Oswestry, the Army having considered him an ideal candidate for the noble art of gunnery.

Malcolm was spared conscription due to having had a mastoidectomy which left him totally deaf in one ear, and on hearing Bunny's tale of woe after he had completed his six weeks of basic training, was relieved to have been spared the ordeal.

Bunny suffered attacks of the Oscar Wilde's, so I will write this as far as possible in Bunny's own style of speech.

My dear boy, you just cannot imagine how totally beastly it was. I caught the train and was surrounded by louts of all shapes and sizes. They said to me, "Are you in the Kate then?" I had not the faintest idea of that which they were asking, and said so. It appeared that 'Kate' was a contraction of Kate Carny which was supposed by them to rhyme with Army.

Having digested this information I concentrated on Mummy's sandwiches which she had, as always, lovingly and thoughtfully provided me.

Eventually the train arrived at the station of Oswestry. My boy, you cannot, even in your most awful dreams, conceive of what followed. A sergeant and two corporals summoned us to attend upon them with the words, "Git over 'ere you load of aunts!"

Bunny never swore, so aunts was the nearest he would go in repeating what they had said, and the last three letters of the word aunt gave enough of what Bunny saw as the very depths of thuggery.

I was expecting a bus or a coach to have met us to convey us to the barracks, my boy. But oh, no! The sergeant and his two cohorts commanded that we run through fairly thick snow, it being February, all the way to these wretched barracks.

On arrival we were shown an iron bed with the aside, "Your bed, right!" and we were then commanded to undress in this unheated room. Then around came a snivelling little private with some large sheets of brown paper. He explained with a smirk on his face that was truly horrible, that we were expected to wrap up our clothes so that they could be "sent 'ome to yer Muvver in that nice 'ouse wiv der blue curtains." We did have blue curtains of course, and I felt tears coming at the recollection. Not that the crawling knave with the paper would have had any sensitivity whatsoever!

It became apparent from the very first that the paper was totally inadequate to cover even my overcoat, and struggle as I might I could not make the ends of the paper cover but the smallest part of this obscene parcel.

After a while the sergeant, seeing that I was in some difficulty, came and watched my struggles. "You're an aunt, whar are yew?" he said. "Yew've got the face of a troublemaker yew 'ave. Well, if it's trouble yew want, trouble yew shall 'ave, and I'm just the bloke to giv it to yer!"

This was the beginning of a beautiful friendship, which was to continue on the next day, but for the last act of the day, just before lights out, poor Bunny was to make one last agonising decision. Since early childhood Bunny had always knelt at the foot of his bed in order to say his night prayers:

> My boy, can you imagine this. Surrounded by these East End thugs I had to kneel and pray. My prayers I am afraid were of very short duration as a hail of pillows descended on me, and I retired to a sleepless night.
>
> Mornings start early, and we were told to don our uniform. Malcolm, it is so very coarse and rough, the very epitome of the life itself! Then in came the sergeant to inform us 'aunts' that we were going 'Ta ta's'! This involved a visit to the camp barber. Well, butcher would have been a better title.
>
> I sat in the chair which was surrounded on all sides by hanks of hair from other poor unfortunates such as myself. The barber enquired as to my former mode of employment, suggesting that I had perhaps been in a bleeding orchestra. He then went through a parody of enquiring how 'Sir' would like it. I mumbled something upon the lines of just tidying it up, whereupon the beast proceeded to cut a great trench from the front of my head to the back. My boy, tears were not far away! I looked at my head in the mirror and was horrified to see a totally bald man looking back at me.

The rest of Bunny's military career ran on very similar lines, he being called a 'great aunt' several times a day. His mother had written to the Queen, the Archbishop of Canterbury, the War Ministry, and anyone else who might have had the slightest influence in order to free Bunny from Hades, but it was all to no avail, and Bunny was forced to complete his statutory two years.

When last heard of he was vicar of a country parish in the wilds of Northumberland, doubtless scarred for life by his military experiences.

Chapter Seven

Our sex education revolved around one of our neighbours who lived in the first house of the next terrace along. He was a most odd looking man due to having a very strange, pale pink, nose. Ian and I were laughing about him one day, and our mother informed us that Dicky Rawlinson had suffered from venereal disease and as a consequence his nose had dropped off, therefore, he had to wear this prosthesis stuck to his face. We were told that if we were promiscuous, the same thing would happen to us. Being quite young at the time, we did not really understand what being promiscuous entailed, but not wishing to appear stupid, did not ask.

Opposite Daphne Lockyer's Post Office was a newsagent's called Flack's who sold a selection of children's toys. Amongst them was a 'disguise set' comprising of a pair of black spectacles with a pale pink nose and black moustache attached. We promptly bought one each and proceeded to give impersonations of Dicky.

Dicky's wife had presumably not been promiscuous because nothing appeared to have dropped off her as far as we could see, but she possessed her own peculiarities. She used to talk as though she was sucking hard on a boiled sweet about every two words. I have since wondered if Victor Borge the musician/comedian had been in conversation with her before writing his Alternative Punctuation skit.

Our window cleaner was a tall, thin man, and on one occasion

Mrs Rawlinson told him that he looked like a man starved. Later that day his wife knocked on her door in a state of high dudgeon, and berated Dickey's wife for insinuating that she starved her husband. "I didn't, th-tut, say he th-tut, was starved, th-tut, I said, th-tut, he looked, th-tut, like a, th-tut, man starved, th-tut." Not impressed with this explanation, the window cleaner's wife smacked Mrs Rawlinson in the mouth and left.

Mrs Shaw lived a few doors up from the Rawlinson's and could be quite rancorous. As a small child, whilst playing ball in the road, Malcolm accidentally kicked it over into her garden. He knocked on her door and asked if he could have the ball back. She sent him home in floods of tears, minus his ball. Dad went hot foot round to her house, his parting words to her being that God would strike her down for being so unkind to a little child.

No sooner had he got back to our house, he heard a crash followed by a blood-curdling scream. It was clearly coming from Mrs Shaw's back garden. Dad returned to her house where he found her with an iron mangle across the top of her feet. The mangle had become dislodged from its stand and had fallen on her.

My father sorely regretted the prophecy of impending doom that he had only minutes before predicted and began to wonder whether he had divine powers!

From that day on poor Mrs Shaw waddled like a penguin and was rather unkindly known as Flatfoot.

Up until his death, screams would also be heard coming from the Webb's house that was next door to Flatfoot Shaw's. Spider Webb, as he was known, suffered from arthritis. His wife used to place brown paper over the affected joints and iron him with a flat iron!

Chapter Eight

My life continued to revolve around horses until I married and my riding activities were put on hold. Five years later I gave birth to our daughter Claire, followed by our son Philip, thirteen months after that.

By the time they were four and five years respectively, we decided to have a complete change of lifestyle, and as Claire had only just started school, decided that was the time to do it. My husband, Chris, had become thoroughly sick of working in London, and I had always wanted to live in Devon where I felt I belonged, so we made our minds up to take the plunge and go.

My beloved mother had died from renal failure a month after Philip was born, so we persuaded my father to consider selling up and moving with us. He was rather unsure at first, but after we had gone, he too moved down, which proved to be the best thing he could have done, as he was able to enjoy the remaining years of his life in Exmouth where he had many happy memories of holidays spent there with my mother and the rest of the family.

For our sins, Chris and I decided to buy a restaurant. This provided three and a half years of drudgery for very little return, but it was a means of moving to a place we had come to love.

The Butler's Pantry was situated in the main street that ran through the town of Budleigh Salterton and was approximately fifty yards from the sea. It was a delightful place to live, being as it was totally unspoilt and within close proximity to the coast and the surrounding countryside. It provided an ideal place for our children to grow up, and despite all the hard work, we have very happy memories associated with Budleigh.

We employed a full-time kitchen assistant. She was a most hardworking person and never complained, but tended to bang and crash about, and would frequently be found standing amongst the ruins of a plate or dish.

When all our electrical appliances were going at once, things got rather hectic. The fish fryer would ring when the contents were cooked, and the chip fryer would buzz. The microwave and toaster would bleep, and if anyone ordered a milkshake it was absolute bedlam. The poor woman would be demented, not knowing which item of food to rescue first, and would turn around in circles until all the bells and whistles had stopped, when she could think straight once again.

She had trouble pronouncing long words. I was knitting a jumper for Philip one day, and not having done very much knitting, was a little confused with the pattern that I was trying to follow. She told me that I must read the 'aggregations'. I immediately twigged that she meant the abbreviations as I had incurred her vocabulary problems before.

One day, whilst doing some shopping in Norman's Cash and Carry, and being the thoughtful person that she was, she rang me up and asked if there was anything we needed whilst she was there. Chris called out that we could do with a bottle of Club Amontillado. Despite knowing full well that I was making a grave mistake in asking her, I said the word very slowly. "WHAT?" she shrieked.

Ten minutes later the dear lady was still trying to pronounce it, until we were both convulsed with laughter and just had to forget about the sherry, and put the telephone down.

Her husband worked as a cleaner at a garage. For some reason I had been under the impression that he was a mechanic, and mentioned this to him one day. Pounding his right temple with his index finger, he informed me that to be a mechanic, "You 'ad to 'ave it up yer, up yer, you 'ave to 'ave it up yer." He continued to repeat these words in his strong West Country accent several times more whilst stabbing at his temple. Eunice, one of our waitresses would wickedly ask him questions that she knew would provoke this response, and would then stand behind him grinning from ear to ear whilst he bashed the side of his head and I struggled to keep a straight face.

Having worked for us for just over two years, this loyal, hardworking lady decided it was time she retired. Her health had been failing and we felt it was a wise decision on her part, although we dreaded the prospect of having to train someone else, as she had come with the restaurant, having been employed by the previous owners, plus the people before them, so she knew the ropes and taught us a lot into the bargain.

She certainly deserved a happy retirement as her life had been far from easy and not without tragedy. She had two sons, one of whom died whilst in his early thirties, and the other was mentally disabled. Her husband of many years died shortly before she retired, but despite everything, she never lost her sense of humour, and was a very lovable person with whom we have stayed in touch to this day.

Eileen was to be our next kitchen assistant. She had been married three times, all with disastrous consequences. The first husband was a farmer. The marriage was stormy but lasted several years due, in no small part, to the fact that it was a large farm, and they were able to stay two hundred acres apart for most of the time. Eileen was a rather impetuous person and did not always think things through. She once borrowed her husband's motorcycle as she desperately needed to get into town. She had seen him start it up, and thought she would be able to handle it. All went well until she tried to stop. Having no idea what the procedure was, she had to ride around until it finally ran out of petrol.

She was an attractive, petite lady in her mid-fifties, extremely well-spoken, and swore like a trooper. I constantly had to remind her about her language as I did not want my children swearing and blinding at the tender ages of six and seven. It transpired that she started to swear soon after joining the Brownies. She was told to bring in some pennies for the Brown Owl, to which Eileen had replied, "Bugger the Brown Owl, let her bring in her own pennies." After that she never changed.

Eileen and I were always laughing about something or other. One day I was talking to a delivery man who delivered bread and cakes to a nearby shop, and always stopped to chat to me if I happened to be outside. Sadly, he had a dreadful stammer, with the letter 'B' being his main stumbling block. On this occasion, in all innocence, I asked him where the bread and cakes were baked. He eventually managed to tell me that the bread was baked in Bradninch. Goodness knows where the cakes came from as I could not spare the time to find out, and hearing Eileen spluttering in the background did not help.

One of Eileen's tasks was to carve the meat. One particular day I had roasted a delicious leg of pork. The smell whilst it was cooking was lovely, and when it came out of the oven it was cooked to perfection with golden brown, crisp crackling, and it was positively mouth-watering. After having slaved over a hot stove all morning, we were both feeling peckish and decided to sample the meat. Eileen, brandishing the carving knife, cut into the succulent pork. Suddenly, there was a loud 'popping' noise followed by the most evil smell. The pig had had an abscess, and Eileen had just lanced it!

Miss Bannister used to lunch at our restaurant each weekday and expected to be served on the stroke of twelve. She had a little schoolroom next door to the Museum in Budleigh Salterton where she taught about eight children, including Claire and Philip, from the ages of five up until they were seven.

Her teaching methods were traditional, and the standard of education that the children received was excellent. She was very firm and stood no nonsense, locking any unruly child in the kitchen until it pleaded for mercy and agreed to give her no more grief.

One of the children had more than her fair share of puppy fat, and Miss Bannister confided in me that she would dearly love to put this child on a bacon slicer.

Miss Bannister was a tiny, frail looking lady, celebrating the evening of her life, although her age was a closely guarded secret. Despite her stature, she was as strong as an ox, thinking nothing of two-mile long nature study walks, rounded off with a game of football in which she participated with gusto, and would return walking briskly along with eight hot, exhausted children trailing miserably along behind her.

She tended her large garden, and would often come in for lunch on Monday covered in scratches and abrasions having spent the weekend taming her rose bushes and shinning up her trees in order to lop off branches.

She would walk down to the little school each day, but occasionally would be seen driving her fairly large car. Due to her small stature, all that could be seen of Miss Bannister was the top of her head.

She once gave a lift to a friend of mine who returned trembling with fright and vowed never to accept a lift with her again.

On the discovery of the pig's abscess, panic set in. A quick trip to Mr Cole the local butcher who used to pronounce turkey as 'toykey', saved the day, and Miss Bannister was served on the stroke of twelve o'clock as usual.

Following her meal, Miss Bannister always ordered coffee which she drank from a small coffee cup. Chris used to pour her coffee, which was quite a challenge as she had a habit of moving the cup and saucer around whilst he was trying to do it, making the task extremely difficult as he had to try and anticipate which way the cup was likely to go before upending the coffee pot. Miraculously, he always managed it without mishap.

One of our customers used to frequent our restaurant each day at 10.15am, to partake of shortbread washed down with a large cup of coffee. She was a large, well-spoken lady who came from a wealthy background and was opposed to wet, cold weather, and was not overly keen on excessive heat, therefore, it was unusual for her ever to be happy with the weather conditions.

Throwing down her oilskins, and vigorously shaking her umbrella one very wet morning, she seated herself down. Eunice, one of our waitresses, greeted her saying, "Good morning," only for the lady to inform her that there was nothing good about it, it was bloody awful.

One summer's day, when the temperature was in the eighties, she got up to depart, and announced to a packed restaurant that she was going home and would be "taking all her clothes orf."

Deciding on what size joint to roast each day was a problem, as we never knew how busy we were likely to be, but we could normally assume that on a hot day people would stay on the beach with a picnic, or just want a light meal rather than a roast dinner. One day, however, we got it totally wrong, and as a hot, sunny day had been forecast, we decided to roast a small joint of lamb. Eileen watched in horror as a coach load of people disembarked outside The Butler's Pantry and filed in. She looked at me in disbelief when told that they had all ordered roast lamb. We stood looking at this miserable piece of meat, and the story of the five loaves and two fishes came to mind. Needless to say, after the initial shock, and an "Oh, shite!" from Eileen, we dissolved into laughter, and somehow managed to eke out the lamb, albeit serving up lifeboat rations.

The hot water supply to our kitchen was provided by an antiquated water heater located over the sink, whose pilot light would blow out if the wind was in a certain direction. Instructions were issued to all staff members that in the event of having to re-light the water heater, they must thoroughly blow out the residue gas first.

One very windy day Eileen obviously did not blow hard enough, resulting in an almighty explosion. I froze to the spot, speechless with horror. After what seemed like an eternity, Rosemary, who was waitressing at the time, who always spoke very slowly and quietly came into the kitchen and whispered, "Are you all right?"

"NO, WE'RE BLOODY WELL NOT!" bellowed Eileen. All the knobs had flown off the water heater, and had landed over the other side of the kitchen into the bowl of scone mix that I had been in the process of making. Signs hanging in the restaurant, namely, Wine by the Glass, No Dogs Allowed Except For the Blind, Cream Teas Served Here and the Open and Closed sign were littered around the restaurant. Fortunately we were closed at the time or someone would have known all about it, especially if the heavy menu case had hit them.

I rarely put in an appearance in the restaurant as I was always knee-deep in flour producing all the food. However, on one of my rare guest appearances I got chatting to a lovely couple on table seventeen. We got onto the subject of weight. I explained that I had a problem and needed to watch what I ate. The gentleman and his wife both looked like a yard of pump water, so I remarked, "I bet you can eat like horses and not put on an ounce." When they had gone, Chris told me that they were called Mr and Mrs Dobbin. I had wondered why Chris and Eunice had made such a hasty exit, now I knew.

Finding the time to take a holiday was always a problem, but when it came to attending funerals we had to make the time. These were the only occasions that we returned to Kent, as generally relatives and friends would visit us.

Aunt Rene died aged eighty-seven in Joyce Green Hospital in Dartford. Her health and sight had been failing for some considerable time, so it was a happy release for her, but a very sad time for my brothers and I as she had been such a wonderful Aunt and Godmother to us. When our mother died aged fifty-nine, Aunt Rene had done her best to step in and fill the gap, making her loss very hard to bear. However, the night before the funeral my brothers, together with our respective husband, wives and children got together for a meal in a restaurant in Sidcup. Not known for a melancholy approach to anything that life threw at us, we celebrated her life in our usual style with much humour.

Some hours and bottles of wine later the waitress delivered the bill to our table. She gave it to Ian who is the 'thespian' of the family. On reading it he promptly clutched at his chest and dramatically fell to the floor where he lay motionless for a few moments. The poor waitress put her hand to her mouth and gasped. Ian then stood up and casually said, "Sorry 'bout that!"

Chapter Nine

We carried out two major changes when we took over The Butler's Pantry. Firstly, we pitched out the old Super Ser that was the only form of heating in the restaurant area as it tended to honk of paraffin and was hardly the focal point of the room. Blue limestone was obtained from the local quarry, and a beautiful, stone fireplace began to take shape. Chris had had a bit of practice at doing this as he had already built one in our previous house. A Jet Master fire was placed in the gap and proved to be extremely efficient. Our regular customers who patronised us throughout the winter months thought it was marvellous, and would spend far more time and money in the establishment as a result.

A dear old couple used to sit on table two which was directly opposite the fireplace, and one particularly cold day, I had a good old stoke up. The flames were shooting out of the coal, and the logs were glowing deep red. The elderly couple turned pink, red, and then puce. I do not know what was throwing out the most heat, them or the fire.

An elderly businessman who frequented our restaurant came in one day to ask if he could possibly book a table for the following Sunday as his sister, who he had not seen for a number of years, was coming over from New Zealand. We did not normally open on Sundays during the winter, but agreed to do this for him. They booked for 1pm by which time the fire was at its best. It could be a bit temperamental on frosty days and grumbled about being lit, displaying its displeasure by smoking and showering the tablecloths with smuts; just in case a dispute with it should arise, it was lit early so that smoke and smuts could be dealt with before any embarrassment was caused.

They all wanted pheasant and some real beauties were obtained, stinking, from Mr Cole the butcher. The cat had the feathers to play with, and our customers had the rest. All was going well. We were complimented on the quality of the food, and congratulated on the fireplace, and told how welcome it was on such a dreary, February day. Then suddenly we noticed the reflection on the wall of blue flashing lights, followed by urgent banging on the side door. I opened the door to be greeted by half a dozen strapping firemen who rushed past me carrying a hosepipe. Not a word was spoken as they made straight for the fireplace and extinguished the fire. We were speechless, and our customers quite taken aback. One of the firemen explained that they had received a call to say smoke was coming out of our restaurant and that the fire was not normally lit on a Sunday, so it was presumed that our chimney was on fire. Not only did they put the dampers on the fire, they also put the dampers on the dinner party!

The other major work to be done was the demolition of the fireplace that was bang in the middle of the kitchen. The kitchen used to be two small rooms, and either side of the fireplace was a two and a half foot gap. This caused total chaos in the kitchen as you could not see who was coming round the corner until you had almost collided with each other, and as we were usually carrying heavy trays of crockery, this was often disastrous.

We tried devising a one-way system, which was to no avail at busy times when we were all running around like headless chickens. We then tried having a demarcation line – kitchen staff one side, waitresses the other. This did not work either, as occasionally waitresses had to come into the kitchen and collect the food because the kitchen staff were too busy to put it through.

After a particularly hot, busy summer, we decided we had had enough of this aggravation, and made plans to demolish the offending article. Chris assured me it would not be difficult and should not take long, but I do not think he bargained for the amount of dust it would create, or the amount of floor space it would take up when spread out in a million pieces. However, after many trips outside to the waiting skip with a wheelbarrow, and much sweeping, the kitchen was transformed. We had closed down for a week to enable us to do the job, and just as well. We could have done with another week off to get over it. The difference it made to the running of the kitchen made it all well worthwhile, and we began to wish we had done it sooner.

When Chris was not reducing the place to rubble, he was growing plants to decorate the restaurant. We had flower troughs dividing up the tables, and window boxes, together with hanging baskets, outside. His favourite flowers were begonias, and the large picture windows seemed to agree with them; they looked quite outstanding.

Every year there was a competition for the best floral display in the town, and in 1982 he won a cup.

Later on that year another competition was held for the best Christmas window display.

Debbie used to do waitressing for us on Saturdays and came in every weekday after school to hoover. She was a lovely girl and a very talented artist. I asked her if she would make a 'stained glass window' effect for the front window of the restaurant. I suggested the Virgin Mary with the baby Jesus as the theme, supplied her with thin, black cardboard and coloured rolls of cellophane paper, and let her get on with it.

The result was absolutely stunning. She had cut the cardboard into a circular shape, and with a craft knife had cut out the shapes of the subjects, then stuck in the cellophane paper. It was quite incredible when viewed, particularly from inside the restaurant with the light behind it, and another prize was notched up.

We lived in the flat that ran above the restaurant, and incorporated the area over the bakery next door, making it a considerable size.

Chris used to produce all the flowers in a greenhouse that he had erected on the patio. Directly opposite the rear of our premises was a block of flats which overlooked the sea, and housed some very unpleasant people.

Following severe gales one night, we got up to find shards of plastic strewn around outside. One of the residents from the flats greeted me with a smug look on her face, and remarked, with unconcealed relish, that our greenhouse appeared to have suffered damage in the storm. As it happened, our greenhouse was unscathed, but part of the roof of the flats had been ripped off. Words cannot describe the pleasure I derived from giving her this information, and seeing the smirk disappear from her face as she hurried back into the damaged building.

I was to nearly reduce another of the rancorous residents to tears when he was extremely rude to my children.

A Resident's Association had been formed within the flats, and the occupants would meet in order to draw up various rules and regulations, usually designed to cause annoyance to someone else.

One of their schemes was to place a large, heavy chain across the entrance into the parking area in front of the flats. This entrance served our restaurant, and neighbouring shopkeepers, and was used daily by delivery men bringing supplies. Much cursing would be heard as they flung the chain away from the entrance before driving in. A resident would sanctimoniously come out and replace the chain, causing further annoyance and delay to the delivery men on their return.

Not only did I have to endure this aggravation, I also had the milkman to contend with. Every morning he would deliver to the flats just before I was due to set out in order to take the children to school. My parking space was just opposite a flight of steps that led into the flats from that side of the building. An identical flight of steps were situated on the other side where no vehicles were parked.

The milkman developed a habit of parking his float directly behind my car, completely boxing me in as a brick wall ran along in front of the car.

On the first occasion that I encountered this problem, I spoke to him, and very politely asked if he would park on the other side.

He did not answer, but I expected him to respect my position, and did not expect the float to be parked there again.

Next morning, my car was once again blocked in by his float. Again I spoke nicely to him, all to no avail as he continued to ignore me. I got fed up with this ridiculous situation and hatched a plan. Prior to his next visit, I moved my car. When he had parked his float, and gone into the flats, I moved the car into position immediately behind his float, blocking him in. I stood leaning nonchalantly against the wall, and on his return commiserated with him about the fact that he could not get out. I told him that I quite understood how he felt, and trusted that he now appreciated my situation and would, in future, park elsewhere.

Unbelievably, next morning my car was again boxed in. I was livid. Climbing into the float, I drove it away, concealing it from view. Going to the foot of the steps, I awaited his return. He descended the steps, and went to fling the empty milk crate onto the float when suddenly he realised that it was not there. Angry as I felt I just had to laugh. His face was a study.

I ceased to have any further problems, as I told him that I would only divulge the whereabouts of his milk float if he promised never to block me in again.

Chapter Ten

After three and a half years of working in the restaurant, Chris decided that he would like to return to engineering. Therefore, when a job was advertised at British Aerospace in Plymouth, he decided to apply, and subsequently got the job. The firm paid for him to relocate, and whilst looking for a house to buy, he was accommodated in a guest house on the Hoe.

Some new houses were being built in Horrabridge that seemed rather nice and within our price range, so we decided to go ahead and buy one. The village was very pleasant with a large park and pretty river running through the centre, and was well equipped with shops and pubs. It was also ideally situated for getting into either Plymouth or Exeter, and handy for buses, trains and aeroplanes. It was on the edge of Dartmoor, which was ideal as we had two chocolate Labradors.

Although we had not sold the restaurant, we decided that we would move all our furniture down to Horrabridge where Chris would live in the house, whilst I continued to run the restaurant whilst we found a buyer. This was a move that I was to regret. The flat above the business was most depressing once void of furniture and the children missed the television and radio. However, I went out and bought a bicycle, and we went out every night cycling.

Eileen lived in a pretty cottage about two miles from the restaurant. She owned a Toggenburg goat called Jane. She used to load Jane into the back of her Morris Traveller and take her up onto Woodbury Common to graze. Knowing the situation in which the children and I were now placed, she would invite us to her cottage where the children would play with Jane, whilst Eileen and I drank gin and tonics. The cycle ride home would be interesting, with the children telling me to stop wobbling about all over the place.

At weekends, either Chris would return to the restaurant, or I would go to Horrabridge. It was much easier for Chris to come home, but the children were excited about the new house, and were keen to go and stay there where they had access to the television once again.

At this time, we had two dogs, two Angora rabbits and a cat. Bertha, our Peugeot 504 family estate, had rusted away, having lived beside the seaside for too long, so we had to cram into Clarence, Bertha's replacement which was a much smaller vehicle. The dogs went in the boot area, the rabbits sat with the children on the back seat, and the cat occupied the front passenger seat incarcerated in a cardboard pet carrier. Claire and Philip always packed enough stuff for a fortnight, although we would only be away for one night, so carrier bags were stacked from floor to ceiling in the back. Dandy, our tabby cat, used to be most put out at having to sit in a cardboard box for an hour, and on one of our journeys decided to escape. The box rolled around on the seat for a while, and then, accompanied by a loud tearing noise, Dandy burst out looking absolutely furious, his ears were sticking out at right angles and his eyes were like saucers. He climbed up onto the dashboard and walked along the ledge until he was standing right in front of my face. This was not ideal as I was travelling fairly quickly down the A38. The children then announced that the rabbits had also got out, and the dogs were trying to get at them. A convenient lay-by saved the day, and somehow we arrived in Horrabridge in one piece.

We eventually sold the restaurant and life returned to normal. Having been rushed off my feet from dawn 'til dusk, I now had to get used to being a lady of leisure. It was all very nice for about a week, and then I started to get itchy feet to do something other than the dreaded housework, and decided it was time to find my piece of land and buy my cow.

At the same time a job was advertised in the *Tavistock Times Gazette* for a Court Usher. Thinking it sounded interesting I successfully applied for the job, and started immediately.

The job entailed working for two days a week, covering Okehampton Court on Thursdays, and Tavistock Court on Fridays, and being available to cover any extra court sittings that were listed.

West Devon Borough Council provided the venue for Okehampton Court, and I enjoyed the twenty minute drive over Blackdown Moor, particularly in springtime as the verges would be lined with snowdrops and primroses, followed by bluebells and campion; plus every other conceivable wild flower that would take their turn to appear, including clumps of daffodils, providing a kaleidoscope of colour.

I would listen to the radio as I rattled along in my old Land Rover, often having the road entirely to myself, and would receive bulletins of traffic jams and public transport problems, never ceasing to give thanks for being so privileged.

Occasionally I would provide a lift to a magistrate or court clerk, and used to feel rather embarrassed at the state of my vehicle as it was frequently used to transport hay and straw, in addition to piglets and calves. With the best will in the world I could not remove all the debris that collected in the nooks and crannies, and bits of hay and straw would be seen sticking up along the channels of the windows. I think people expected to see Worzel Gummidge clamber out rather than a smartly dressed woman.

We frequently dealt with cases concerning farmers entailing unburied carcasses, cruelty, pollution of water courses and such like. The press would invariably attend, and I would be filmed driving along Oaklands Road towards the court as they presumed that I was the defendant. They received quite a surprise when I alighted with as much decorum as my skirt would allow, and they would shamble off to await the arrival of another Land Rover. If they were unlucky, and the defendant arrived in an ordinary car, thus giving them the slip, I would see my Land Rover on the local *Spotlight* news as they used me as a substitute.

The most embarrassing incident was when I was required to attend a course along with other court staff that was being held at the Riviera Centre in Torquay. Coaches had been organised to transport us from Plymouth, and we were due to leave from Plymouth Magistrates' Court car park at 8am. Mary, who worked in the court office in Tavistock, offered me a lift into Plymouth which I was more than happy to accept as my Land Rover was looking worse than usual having delivered two piglets to someone the day before, and I had not had the opportunity to clean the vehicle out.

At 7am, on the day, I received a frantic telephone call from Mary. Her car would not start. Taking a deep breath I told her that I was on my way. I was wearing a suit, the skirt of which was fairly tight and was not the ideal attire for climbing up into Landy. After a considerable struggle I was eventually seated behind the wheel and furiously driving towards Tavistock as time was, by now, getting on.

Mary was waiting on the pavement wearing an even tighter skirt than mine, and minced towards the Land Rover on six inch stilettos. Memories of my beloved mother trying to get into Malcolm's Austin Healy Frogeye Sprite came flooding back as Mary debated the best way to climb in. I was of no help whatsoever as it had taken me all my time to get in, and being convulsed with laughter compounded the problem. Thankfully, the pavement was a little higher further along the road, so I drove along, with Mary wobbling along beside me, to this point where she finally managed to scramble in.

The Plymouth Magistrates' Court has its own underground car park, and on our arrival two attendants were supervising the parking, checking that only court personnel were admitted. If it had not been for Mike Johnston, a court clerk with whom I had worked for many years, I think we would have been turned away. He came up to Landy grinning from ear to ear. On seeing the straw protruding from various gaps in the bodywork and window frames, he remarked that some things did not change. He assured

Me with my trusty Landrover – 'Landy'.

The barn prior to renovation.

Mary and Martha.

Mountaineering Monty with Mary looking on.

Chris renovating the barn.

Beefy and Clover as calves.

Clover aged one year.

Bluebell aged two days.

The incorrigible Albert!

Rosebud, our first South Devon.

Poppy and Moses.

Violet and Buttercup.

Lady, Susie and Topsy doing their version of an advert for butter!

Suki.

Polly.

the attendants that we were connected with the court, and we were dubiously allowed in.

Then the problem as to how we were going to extract ourselves from the vehicle arose.

The coaches were twenty minutes late in leaving with Mary and me, who were, needless to say, last to board, receiving a few black looks.

Tavistock Court was a purpose-built courthouse situated in Bedford Square. Constructed of light grey granite, it is a most imposing looking building with castellated towers on the roof, and dates back many years.

The main courtroom was styled on a similar room in the Old Bailey, and was quite awesome with the Scales of Justice on the wall above the head of the Chairman of the Bench, with colourful plaques either side bearing the mottos: *Honi soit qui mal y pense*, and *Che sarà sarà*.

The press sat in the area that appeared to have been used for a jury in days gone by, and names of reporters were carved into the top of the desk dating back to the 1920s. Normally only one reporter from the *Tavistock Times Gazette* was present, but if we were dealing with a case that drew a lot of media attention, it could be packed.

Leading down from the dock was a narrow, winding staircase that led to what can best be described as a rabbit-warren. Little passages wound their way around beneath the court and adjoining police station where the old cells were located.

In order to get a feel for how it must have been for a prisoner incarcerated in one of these cells, I went in and closed the heavy, solid oak door behind me. It was pitch black with no windows save for a slit high up in the wall, and was barely four feet square. The floor comprised of granite flagstones which would have added to the prisoner's misery as this was all there appeared to be to sit on. It was freezing cold and damp in there, so I did not stay long, and quickly headed back up the stairs with a prickly sensation on the back of my neck, and a creepy feeling that I was not alone.

The modern cells were quite different, being light and airy,

f

complete with a long, hard wooden bench, and a toilet. A blanket was folded up at one end of the bench making it seem positively cosy by comparison to the old cells; but again, I did not choose to tarry.

Various little rooms that led off from the passageway were used for interviewing, fingerprinting and photograph taking, and such like. The passageway finally led up into the police station. This is an antiquated building which reminded me of the television programme, *Heartbeat*. I used to half expect to see Ventris sitting there rather than a civilian desk clerk.

Court Two was a simple affair, being a fairly large room with what appeared to be old church pews for seating. An enormous, solid oak table with ornate carvings on the legs and drawer fronts was set in front of an open fireplace where the magistrates' would sit, with the court clerk on one end and the defendant sitting opposite. The fire surround was highly decorative, if not rather blackened from when it had been used in past times.

The walls were bedecked with photographs of clerks and magistrates dating back to the late 1800s, and held a great fascination for me.

I would need to ply between the two courtrooms as I was the only usher, and by the end of the session I would feel quite tired. The building was not 'user friendly' as there were steps and stairs all over the place, including a spiral staircase that led up into the Magistrates' Retiring Room, and this partly led to its very unfortunate closure on 15th December, 2000.

I did not work on this day as Chris, Claire and I were at Sandhurst watching the Passing Out Parade in which Philip was taking part. By all accounts it was a sad day, with people from all sectors within the court service making speeches, leaving everyone straining to keep a stiff, upper lip.

Tavistock is now bereft of a courthouse, with people having to travel into Plymouth, and a beautiful, historic building is being left to decay.

Camborne had what can only be described as 'an apology' for a courthouse. Various organisations used the facilities, including a local drama group who staged annual pantomime's there.

One day, around Christmas time, I was talking to a solicitor who had, the previous day, conducted a trial in Camborne Court. He told me that the case had been a difficult one, and that he had spent the entire day addressing the magistrates' who were sat "beneath Jack's bloody Beanstalk!" He certainly shed no tears when that court was closed down.

Chapter Eleven

As I was only the usher, the defendants felt able to talk to me enabling me to have an opportunity of trying to talk some sense into them. Affectionately known to them as 'Batwoman' because of my black cloak, they would talk freely to me, and occasionally heeded my advice.

I used to get quite upset if I had not seen someone for some considerable time, only for them to arrive at court for committing another offence. I expressed my dismay at seeing one young man with whom I had developed a good rapport, only for him to say, "Yeah, life's a bitch, innit?" and proceed to laugh his head off. For him arrest was merely an occupational hazard, but he never bore any malice towards court officials, and accepted his punishments with a good grace, even when told he would be kept at Her Majesty's pleasure. Her Majesty was to have the pleasure on many occasions.

We had a diamond thief attend one day on the arm of a policeman. He looked such a nice, respectable gentleman, wearing a nice, light suit with a panama hat. He had gone into a jeweller's in Okehampton and asked to see a tray of rings, which he then grabbed and headed for the door, but sadly for him, the jeweller was quite fleet of foot and managed to grab him, rings and all.

It transpired that he was wanted all over the world for theft of precious stones, and it seemed rather amusing that he was finally apprehended in a sleepy little backwater in Devon.

Court clerks came in an assortment of personalities, one of which was quite eccentric. He had retired just before I started work there, but stories of him were legendary. "Which side of the bed do you want?" he would demand of any pretty female who was about to seat herself at the table.

On one occasion he was dealing with a case of the possession of an offensive weapon. The weapon in question was a lethal looking dagger and looked extremely offensive. However, the solicitor acting on behalf of the equally offensive looking defendant argued that it was not an offensive weapon. Upon hearing this, the clerk picked up the dagger and plunged it into the top of the table where it quivered whilst he proclaimed that it looked offensive enough to him.

Thankfully, the defendant was not asked to give a demonstration as to how he had used the offending article, unlike the case of a fairly elderly defendant who had attacked his neighbour with a telescopic baton.

A dispute involving car parking had arisen between the two neighbours, and the defendant was asked to give an account of the events that had taken place. Seizing hold of the baton, he proceeded to flail it about in all directions, missing both myself and the prosecutor by a cat's whisker. He was quickly assured by the Chairman of the Bench that they had a clear picture of what had happened, thank you very much, and the baton was confiscated and tactfully placed well out of his reach!

Emotions would run high in certain cases, particularly offences involving paedophiles and arsonists, when members of the public would turn up intent on hurling abuse and punches at defendants arrested on charges of this nature.

On one occasion, a man was led into court handcuffed to a police officer, and wearing a paper suit, having tried to set fire to his house whilst his wife and children slept upstairs. Due to shortages of police officers that day, the poor constable had no back up and had to cope as best he could. On arrival he was greeted with jeers, but on the way out a few more people had gathered and the officer was knocked flying, and the defendant was duffed up, leaving his paper suit in ribbons. The mob shuffled off, clearly satisfied at the summary justice that they had meted out.

On occasions, defendants would become violent whilst having their cases dealt with, especially if they were told that they were to go to prison. One of our clerks sustained a graze to his arm when the little wooden door that separated him from the defendant was kicked in, sending shards of wood flying straight at him. An extra month was immediately added to his custodial sentence.

Defendant's approach to a court appearance differed enormously. Some would dress very smartly in suits, whilst others would wear nice casual clothes. The regular attendants wore jeans and sweatshirts, often with logos and artwork printed on their backs.

A well-built lady turned up one day with 'WIDE LOAD' emblazoned across her ample bosom, taking the ribald comments from her fellow defendants in her stride.

A female magistrate arrived on one occasion sporting a sweatshirt. I think she had decided to follow the advice of 'if you can't beat 'em, join 'em'. The shirt bore a nautical design, and printed over the top of the ropes and rowlocks were the words, 'WRECKED AGAIN'. On this occasion she was having what is commonly known as a bad hair day coupled with a troublesome bunion that had required a slit to be made in the side of her shoe in order to let it out. As she sat at the bench, the sweatshirt creased, leaving only part of a word showing. The word was 'WRECK'.

I had had the privilege of working with some really lovely people. In addition, despite their crimes, I had an affection for a lot of our 'clients'. It had been a demanding but rewarding job, and a feeling of bereavement came when, as I have already mentioned, Tavistock Court was closed, allegedly to save money, and I was made redundant. It was a devastating experience after having spent fifteen happy years in a most unique and interesting job.

Chapter Twelve

It was shortly after starting my job that I was, at last, to realise my lifelong ambition, and buy my piece of land.

The field was advertised in the *Western Morning News* which I had been scanning for weeks in the hope of something turning up. I could not believe my eyes when I found the advert for the four acres of land in Horrabridge. Never in my life have I been in such a state, and had to insist that Chris rang the number given as I was far too wound up to hold a sensible conversation. Telling me to calm down, he picked up the telephone. All I could hear was, "Yes, yes. Oh, right, yes. Oh, I see, yes." This went on for what seemed like an eternity, by which time I was nearly climbing the walls. When he finally put the telephone down, and told me where the field was, I bolted straight out of the door to the car.

It was a typical, miserable November day, and pouring with rain, but the field looked beautiful. In the corner was a building made from scaffold boards and baler cord. An old, blue up and over garage door graced the front, together with delights such as pallets and rusty corrugated sheets. Inside there was dung, dung, and more dung, plus some old furniture, including a rickety dining chair that I was to use later when milking a Jersey cow that we were to acquire. One side of the barn was virtually non-existent as the corrugated sheets had rusted away leaving jagged holes.

Undaunted by the state of the place, we resolved to turn it into first class housing for the animals that we planned to get, and returned home in order to ring the owner and make an offer. The offer was accepted and within a week, despite not having exchanged contracts, we furnished it with a dozen hens. They were point of lay, and gave us good service up until a fox paid us a visit and killed every single one, leaving them intact, and surrounded in feathers. It was most distressing, and seemed so unnecessary as he obviously was not hungry. As time went by we had to learn to live with these unfortunate events, the hardest of all being the demise of poor Martha.

Martha was given to us, together with Mary, by our local vicar. His wife was a schoolteacher in the village, and one day one of her little pupils announced that her mummy had to get rid of two goslings. Phyllis, in her ignorance, thought how lovely it would be to have them, and duly went home to twist her husband's arm into letting her keep them. He rather begrudgingly agreed, and set about making a small run in the garden. The goslings arrived, and in an incredibly short space of time, had reduced the run to a stinking quagmire. They decided that the goslings would have to go, and wasting no time, Geoff turned up on our doorstep with them in a cardboard box and begged us to give them a home, quickly departing before we could say whether we wanted them or not. They turned out to be tremendous characters, and we got very attached to them.

About three years later, tragedy struck. Mary and Martha were paddling in the stream that ran along the bottom of the field as was their custom, when a dog fox plus a vixen came on the scene. Martha was seized moments before we got near enough to do anything, and between them they tore her in half.

Poor Mary was devastated at losing her sister, so we decided to buy a gander for her. Monty arrived within a week. She seemed to approve of him, and they became inseparable. When Mary came into lay, he would turn from being a docile bird into a delinquent, his hobbies changing from grass eating and preening to vandalism and grievous bodily harm. A stick had to be carried whenever he was in the vicinity or severe bruising to the arms and legs was guaranteed. The loose skin on the backs of our hands was one of the worst places to receive a nip as it was extremely painful. Chris made sure that he would not get him again in this area, and armed himself with a broom handle before making any contact with Monty.

The gander was keen on climbing and would awkwardly clamber up onto anything that happened to be lying around. One evening he came limping across the field looking very sorry for himself. Pulling on a pair of gauntlet-styled gardening gloves, Chris lifted him up so that I could inspect his legs and feet. He had managed to lacerate the skin between two of his toes, leaving a claw nearly hanging off. Having no idea as to what to do we decided that he would have to see a vet.

Sitting in the veterinary surgery just after Christmas with a goose on my lap caused considerable amusement, and many comments came in my direction from people nursing puppies and kittens. Even the vet was grinning from ear to ear, until Monty grabbed the loose skin on the back of his hand. However, the surgeon got even with the bird by cutting off the damaged toe, leaving Monty with a permanent limp.

Mary did succeed in producing some goslings, but sadly something took them one night. We were gutted, as hatching goslings is quite a feat, and we have not had any since although Mary patiently sits on her eggs every year, and Monty continues to beat us up.

Having at least got a few birds on the place, we decided to attack the barn in preparation for the larger animals we intended to keep. We stood and looked at it wondering where on earth to start. Chris said we should take a bulldozer to it, but I argued that it would take far too long to start from scratch, and having already waited thirty-three years, I decided that was long enough and I was not prepared to wait any longer, so a good bodge-up had to be planned.

We first set about clearing the dung with fork and barrow. This took some considerable time. The worst areas were under the bits of roof that leaked, thus reducing the dung to slurry. This was a shovel job rather than fork, but whether on the end of a fork or shovel made no difference to the smell which was evil. Eventually we became accustomed to it, and it did not seem quite so bad. The main perpetrators of the awful smell had been sheep with an occasional bullock thrown in. Apart from pig plops, sheep droppings take some beating in the stink stakes.

However, we bravely soldiered on, our thoughts trained on the vision of dear little calves lying in the pens contentedly chewing the cud, and before too long the place was spotless and sweet smelling, and the field fertilised organically with SH – 1T instead of non-organic 20-10-10. Pesticides and fertilisers were things we intended to avoid as we felt the planet was damaged enough already without us adding to the pollution. We were told by other farmers that we would not get grass without it, but we did, and all the animals thrived.

Having got to the point where we could see the floor, we started wondering what to do with the front and sides. Once again, our trusty local paper came to our aid with an advertisement for a log cabin. It was on a holiday home site in Challaborough together with several others, and it was down to the buyer to dismantle and collect. My friend Glen Robinson's husband, Mark, agreed to help us as he was a builder, and arrived on the site with a hammer, claw-bar, and a suitable vehicle with which to take it away. Our contribution was a bottle of lemonade and as much strength as we could muster.

Mark wasted no time, and was on the roof in a trice. The noise was deafening. Wood and roofing felt came raining down, and in record time it was completely flattened. Then came the hard bit, trying to get it on the flat-bed lorry. It was so heavy and awkward, but somehow we got it loaded, and gingerly drove off leaving a bare patch of ground where it had once housed many people enjoying a holiday under its roof. One could almost hear the excited cries of little children arriving on the site and seeing this lovely log cabin overlooking the sea, and feel their delight at being able to live in it for a couple of weeks, their imaginations running riot.

It looked anything but lovely now; in fact I began to have grave doubts about ever being able to reconstruct it, as most of the noise during its demolition was that of tearing wood that gave out a sound that indicated it was now beyond repair. Desperate for a cup of tea, we parked up outside our house, log cabin and all. Refreshed from the tea, we drove up to the field, hoping and praying that the cargo would not slide off on the steep bit of the lane, and would go in through the gate when we reached the field. Fortunately, all went well, and we parked as near to where we wanted to put the pieces of cabin, and began heaving and hauling for all we were worth. By this time I think we could have cheerfully put a match to it as the thoughts of handling it all over again were not pleasant to say the least. However, after a few days regaining our strength, we started dismantling the front of the barn ready to replace with bits of log cabin. Several hours of hard labour went into this, but the result was very rewarding, particularly when it was rounded off with a lick of creosote. The old garage door was replaced with stable doors made from scaffold boards, and the whole front was transformed.

That completed, and a new roof put on the leaky end, it was now ready for the calves. I decided it would be a good idea to go on a course in order to learn about looking after calves, having already arranged to buy two from a farm near Truro. "Putting the cart before the horse again," grunted Chris. I cannot deny that I have a habit of doing this, and just said that I did not want to change a habit of a lifetime.

I contacted Bicton College of Agriculture and arranged to go on a course the following weekend. Clover and Beefy arrived on Friday and I went away on the Saturday, staying overnight, and returning on the following evening. My dear friend, Glen Robinson agreed to assist Chris with them while I was away. She had reared calves in the past, and knew a bit about it. It seemed a bit of a cheek leaving her to get on with it like this, but she was delighted as she and I are kindred spirits, and she had also wanted to own a cow, but unfortunately had not had the opportunity. So off I went leaving milk powder, calf pellets and numerous instructions. The course proved to be very informative, but also frightened me to death. I went in November on a damp, drizzly, humid day, only to be told this was ideal weather for calves to get pneumonia. I spent the weekend having visions of Clover and Beefy being half dead from it on my return, and poor Glen beside herself thinking it was something she had done wrong. We also learned about scour, and how some calves do not recover from this. I began to get the impression that whatever you did was likely to cause death, and began to have doubts about my ability to rear calves. A vet was in attendance, and demonstrated de-horning, and then asked if anyone would like to have a go. Everyone took a step back except me who volunteered. I think seeing him inject anaesthetic just above the eyes of the calf, and explaining that you have to be accurate as to where you place the needle put them off, but I felt confident about this, and made a successful job of it. He also taught us restraining techniques, and gave us a wealth of valuable information.

A man from ADAS was also in attendance, and advised on housing, stressing the importance of ventilation in the calf house. He got quite carried away drawing arrows illustrating air-flow. They seemed to point every which way until I was totally confused as to where air was supposed to be coming from, or where it was supposed to be going. I just crossed my fingers and hoped our log cabin was going to do the trick.

We were taught about Barley Beef, and taken on a tour of their farm. The bulls fed on barley were like the sides of houses. Their heads were absolutely enormous, and they looked quite frightening. Only a single metal bar was between them and us, and I could not help wondering, if they decided to pit their strength against the metal bar, who would come out best. Fortunately they seemed more interested in their food than us which was a mercy.

We moved to another section where cattle were reared in a different way. Their figures were a lot trimmer, and they looked much friendlier. All in all it was an enjoyable and interesting course which was to stand me in good stead.

When I got home on the Sunday evening, I was relieved to find the calves alive and well. Chris and Glen had coped very well, and Glen said she would be only too pleased to help out at any time as she had thoroughly enjoyed the experience.

Chapter Thirteen

Clover was a week old Friesian heifer, and Beefy a Hereford X bull calf of the same age. Clover was the boss from the word go, and Beefy really had to watch his step, which did not bother him in the least as he was a very laid back animal, and was quite prepared to let her rule the roost. Chris laboured hard and long in providing five-star accommodation for them, only to be thanked by Clover scaling the partition and disappearing out of the barn and into the field. We did not actually see her do it, we simply felt the draught as she sailed past. We were to learn a lot of lessons in pen construction over the next few years, particularly when we ventured into pigs.

My eldest brother, Malcolm, together with Dawn, his wife, were holidaying in Devon at the time we turned the calves out after the winter, and paid us a visit as they were keen to see the smallholding that I had been threatening to start up for so many years. Malcolm enquired as to what I proposed to do with them. I told him that I was going to milk Clover and eat Beefy. "What if, when you die, you find that God's a bullock?" he laughingly said, and went on laughing and joking until the calves decided to come over and see us. They ran flat out across the field, heading straight for us, thus frightening the life out of Malcolm. Knowing them as we did, we would just stand still whilst they whizzed by. However, my brother did not have sufficient faith in me when, as they came charging towards us, I told him simply to stand his ground, and he made the decision that before they got any closer, he would make a run for it. Apart from Linford Christie, I have never seen anyone cover so much ground in such a short space of time. He was across the field and over the gate like something possessed, much to Clover's disappointment, as she had been so enjoying the chase.

The calves were thrilled to bits at having their new found freedom, and although Beefy was content to munch grass, then lie down and quietly chew the cud, Clover had other ideas of how to spend her time. Eroding the stone wall hedging with her head was one pastime, leaving the white areas on her face plastered in red Devon soil, and a pile of stones at her feet for us to have to reinstate. She was quite a character in her way.

Malcolm and Dawn never visited our farm again, and took their holidays elsewhere!

When Clover was two and a half years old, we had her AI'd to an Aberdeen Angus. This was successful, and she presented us with the sweetest little black calf. It was the size of a small Labrador. We had stayed with Clover constantly as the calving time drew near, and were choked with emotion when Bluebell finally appeared. Clover looked extremely pleased with herself, and dutifully washed her calf, mooing and fussing over it like an old hen. All went well until Bluebell decided it was time to go in search of the milk bar. Clover was having none of it. Up came a back leg which shot out like a piston aimed directly at poor Bluebell who ended up over the other side of the pen looking quite shaken up. Clover was severely reprimanded, Bluebell retrieved and put back to the udder ready for a repeat performance. We began to get desperate. We had a cow bursting with milk, and a starving calf, but all attempts at getting the two together seemed totally impossible.

Albert White, a retired farmer friend, was summoned to attend in order to advise on the best way forward. He came with prophecies of impending doom. The cow was going to get mastitis. The calf was going to die, etc., etc., and then he finally suggested getting an older calf to put on her. We frantically telephoned round neighbouring farmers to see if anyone would sell us a calf, and very fortunately obtained Tulip, a Limousin X. Limousins are tough little beggars, and Tulip was no exception. Although only two weeks old, she knew what she wanted, and nothing or no one was going to stand in her way of getting it, and on arrival she wanted milk. Poor Clover wondered what had hit her. Her own calf had given up all hope of getting a feed, and had curled up in a corner as far away from her mother as she could possibly get. Tulip made a dive straight for the teat. Seeing this huge bag of milk must have made her think it was Christmas, and having got hold of a teat there was no way she was going to let go. Clover was doing the Highland Fling while Tulip hung on for grim death, slurping away, milk running down either side of her mouth, her feet firmly planted in the straw. As soon as she had emptied one teat, she was onto another in a flash. Clover began to realise that she had been outdone, and decided to stand still and think of England. Tulip slurped her way through all four teats, then looking positively rotund, went over and joined Bluebell. A little later we reintroduced Bluebell to the teat, and apart from the odd kick, Clover succumbed, and Bluebell got her tea.

However, Clover never fed the calves with a good grace, and even Tulip was knocked for six on one occasion. She got up, momentarily dazed, regained her sea-legs, and waded into the milk more determined than ever to suck the old baggage dry. Bluebell used to hang back and wait for Tulip to get started and take the worst of the blows, and then she would sneak up the back and grab a teat from between the hind legs, thus keeping out of the line of fire. Both calves grew well as Clover had no shortage of milk even if she had a shortage of temper. Initially, after being milked, she would eye the calves with disdain, but after a while she would proffer her tongue and give Bluebell a quick lick, albeit half-heartedly.

Poor Clover was only to have one more calf. This was Bovril, an enormous bull calf. Again Clover decided mothering was definitely not her forte, and proceeded to knock seven bells out of Bovril, but he was standing for none of it and, like Tulip before him, took hold of the teat, and hung on regardless of the mêlée breaking out around him.

When Bovril was a year old, Clover began to change. Her personality seemed different. I could not explain it, but she just was not the same. Then, one day, I approached her in the field, and she did not seem to know I was there. Her eyes were glazed and her back slightly arched. I waved my hand in front of her face, but she did not respond, then suddenly she jumped, like someone being awakened abruptly from sleep, and looked at me in a surprised way. I racked my brains as to what could be wrong, but apart from the fact that I had recently wormed her with Ivomectin, could think of nothing that could have caused her to ail. A few days later she seemed unsteady on her feet, sort of trembly. By now I felt sick as I began to feel sure she had BSE. I had got a vet to have a look at her when I first noticed a change in her, but she could find nothing obvious, and just said to keep an eye on her. This time I called the Ministry of Agriculture. They sent a vet who put her down, removed her head, and sent it away for examination, and a few weeks later I received a postcard informing me that she had tested positive for BSE.

Bovril did not seem to miss Clover, which was not surprising as she had not exactly doted on him, and by now he was weaned and independent.

About six months following the death of Clover, I found Bovril lying down, looking very ill. His temperature was sky high and his eyes looked glazed. I froze to the spot feeling convinced that he too had BSE. I seized a towel, soaked it in cold water, and put it on his head. He appeared to appreciate this cold compress, so I continued to try and cool him in this way. When he felt cooler, I rushed home and called the vet. He could not diagnose the problem, but did not think it was BSE. However, as a precaution, he called in the Ministry vet. By the time she arrived, Bovril's eyes had turned white and he was totally blind. The vet insisted that he be driven out into the field, much to my annoyance. I remonstrated with her, but she still proceeded to drive him around whilst he stumbled and bumped into things. She then announced that she did not know what was wrong, but was certain that it was not BSE as he was too young at eighteen months to have it. I argued that it was my understanding that it was possible for the mother to transmit the disease, but I think at the time so much money was being used to compensate farmers for BSE casualties, it was not a good idea to admit that Bovril had it, thus making a complete and utter nonsense of the investigation that was being carried out.

I begged the vet to put Bovril down immediately to spare him any more suffering, but she told me that she was not paid to go around putting animals down for people. I made it clear that if I ever saw her again it would be too soon.

I had Bovril destroyed shortly after her departure, and a few more tears were shed.

Chapter Fourteen

The South Devon's read like a passage from the Old Testament in my Herd Book. Rosebud begat Poppy, Poppy begat Daisy, Daisy begat Marigold and so on until there were twelve. All the girls were named after flowers. The boys were given ordinary names to avoid them getting an inferiority complex, apart from Sweet William.

Rosebud was bought from Patrick Toop who owned a large farm in Yelverton and bred the most beautiful South Devon cattle. His father, Dick, had farmed the land before him, and when Dick retired, our friend, Albert, pulled his leg about being idle. Dick replied that if the farm could not support one lazy bugger, it was a poor show.

Rosebud grew to be enormous. She was quiet and gentle, and loved to be groomed and petted. She was AI'd to a Hereford, and produced Poppy who looked like her father, but had Rosebud's temperament. We used to milk her, and enjoyed the most delightful, creamy puddings. Poppy in turn was AI'd to a South Devon, and gave birth in the leat that runs from Plaisterdown along the bottom of our field.

Albert was employed as midwife on that day. I had to go to work as the calving fell on a Friday, that being Tavistock Court day. Having checked her first thing in the morning, I felt that calving was imminent. Albert was summoned, and parked his Land Rover in the field where he stayed the whole time and kept watch. He was unable to prevent Poppy from going down into the leat to give birth, and had to pull the calf out of the water, hence I named him Moses. Not best pleased at getting his boots and trouser legs wet, Albert named him something else, implying that he did not have a father. Moses was the image of his mother, and again had a kind, gentle nature.

Most of our cattle were produced on our holding, but I did buy the occasional calf from Hatherleigh Market which I hand reared and kept until it was about two and a half years old. If the calf was a Hereford X, I would sell it on to Philip Cole, a neighbouring farmer, as a herd replacement.

I loved rearing the calves by hand, and even now I am never happier than when I am teaching them to drink from a bucket, my hand in the warm milk holding onto the teat that they suck the milk through, gradually withdrawing the teat until their mouths are in the milk. I tell them it is as easy as riding a bike, and they soon catch on.

My friend Wendy Eldridge's parents owned Grimstone Farm which was situated close by. Her father, John Rowe, kept a beautiful South Devon bull called Trewint Sunshine who was father to some of our calves. When John retired, I bought a lovely South Devon cow at his sale. She was named Grimstone Jean after John's wife. I renamed her Violet so that she did not feel the odd one out.

Violet was in calf when I bought her, and produced a beautiful heifer that we named Buttercup. When Buttercup was just over a year old, I decided to take Violet to meet her new husband who lived over Plaisterdown. The farm was within walking distance, so Chris and I set off with Violet, and took little Buttercup along as well as she did not seem too keen on being separated from her mother.

The journey turned out to be an absolute fiasco. First of all, Violet decided that she did not want to go. A bucket of cow cake was dangled in front of her causing her to have a change of heart, so off we went. At the other end of the lane is a large, old manor house, together with a mews. Grimstone Manor is used for various 'workshops' and a lot of people congregate there, and in the summer months sunbathe in the grounds. On this day a lady was sunbathing in the garden beside the mews. Unfortunately, she had left the little gate open that leads out into the lane. By the time we had reached this point, Violet had lost interest in the cow cake, and was taking stock of her new surroundings. On seeing the gate, she charged through with Buttercup close on her heels, frightening the life out of the poor woman who was wearing very little, and demolishing a large quantity of flowers. She was like the proverbial bull in the china shop, ploughing up the lawn, and flattening everything in sight.

Finally, after many apologies to the scantily clad woman who did not know where to put herself, we proceeded uneventfully past the manor house, and on into Jordan Lane which led up to the moor. On seeing the vast expanse of moorland before them, Violet and Buttercup became very frisky, and trotted off at an alarming pace, with Chris and me running after them. At this time, Chris suffered attacks of paroxysmal tachycardia, and just to add to our problems, had an attack. Very fortunately, Wendy Eldridge was out on her horse, Mister, and cantered over to assist. She rounded up the two beasts, and after that things went smoothly.

Violet was introduced to the bull, and left, together with Buttercup, for three weeks, during which time we hoped she would conceive.

However, most unfortunately, it transpired that Violet was not in calf, but little Buttercup was. This was a disastrous situation, and by the time we realised what had happened, we could do nothing but hope the calf would be small. However, this was not to be, and an enormous bull calf was born dead. Philip Cole, together with his father Bill, had very kindly come over to assist with the calving, and they were both so upset. They took the calf away for me, sparing me any more distress.

Apart from this episode, all our other calvings went smoothly. It was getting some of the mothers to accept and suckle their offspring that was sometimes a problem, but I was well versed in the procedure thanks to Clover, and equipped myself with an anti-kicking device which I put on the recalcitrant cow, thus solving the problem.

The next wrench was parting with the calves having devoted so much time to them and becoming very attached to them.

I had three Charolais X calves that I purchased from Lindsey Rogers, another neighbouring farmer. Lindsey farmed along the Whitchurch Road at Sortridge Farm. He was always very kind and helped us with our hay-making on occasions. The farm was a dairy farm, and Lindsey would take the calves away from their mothers soon after they were born, and rear them on. It was fatal for me to go and see the calves because I would never return home empty handed, and on one occasion Lady, Susie and Topsy accompanied me home. They were irresistible with their cream coats and pretty little faces. I took a lot of stick over these calves as I had always maintained that I would never have a Charolais because they were French, and I felt the meat was inferior to British breeds.

When they were about a year old I decided to sell them on. As Philip Cole only kept Hereford crosses, he was not interested in them as herd replacements, and so I took them over to Hatherleigh Market. By now I had my own trailer which was made for me by the multi-talented Stuart Davey who was caretaker at Tavistock Police Station.

Lady, Susie and Topsy went happily up the ramp as it was not too steep or slippery, and a deep bed of straw awaited them. The trailer had four wheels making the ride extremely comfortable for them.

Once at the market they were herded into a pen. I had a lump in my throat big enough to put in a wheelbarrow at seeing them looking so bewildered. A café provided some solace with bacon 'butties' and hot mugs of tea. It seems the first thing we Brits do in times of adversity is to have a cup of tea.

The larger animals were sold first, followed by the calves. Mine did not go into the ring for some considerable time, and by the time they did, I was a nervous wreck. A dealer bought them, and I had reservations as to how well they would be treated from then on, and decided there and then that I wanted them back.

I approached the auctioneer who was very nice about it, but explained that once he had knocked them down to the purchaser, there was nothing he could do, but suggested that I approach the man who had bought them and ask if I could have them back.

Dear Albert had accompanied me to the sale, and he approached the dealer waving a twenty pound note. The dealer grudgingly agreed to return the calves to me and snatched the money. His attitude confirmed that I was right about not letting him have them.

Looking quite dazed by their ordeal, the calves gratefully clambered back into the trailer, and home we went.

After keeping them for a bit longer, I sold them on to a private purchaser where I felt sure they would continue to be kept in the manner to which they had become accustomed.

From then on I only produced meat for our freezer as I could not possibly go through an experience like that again.

Polly and Suki were purchased at the Dartmoor Prison farm sale that takes place every year, usually in October. Princetown is a bleak, miserable looking place at the best of times, therefore, the grey stone prison buildings do it no favours.

The pubs and restaurants thrive during the summer months in the God-forsaken place due not only to their close proximity to the moor, but by tourists' fascination with the prison. A small lay-by provides a perfect spot for viewing this granite fortress, and many a traffic jam is created as a result on the normally deserted road.

The farm sale is held some distance away from the actual prison, so one is unable to see prisoners peering out from behind bars. The sale is usually well attended with buyers coming from all over the country due to the quality of the animals that are produced there; that is with the exception of the two Aberdeen Angus heifers that I bought.

The day of the sale dawned cold, wet and grey which is typical in Princetown. The animals were penned up outside in the fog, whilst the farmers were under cover in a huge barn arranged with tiers of straw bales to provide seating for when the sale got underway. A temporary sale ring was placed opposite the bales, with a narrow runway leading from the pens outside. Prior to the auction you could have a good look at the animals, if you could see through the mist that hung like a veil in front of them, and make a note of their numbers that were stuck with glue to their flanks, before the bidding started.

Several black calves were for sale, but according to the catalogue, only two were Aberdeen Angus. Not having the faintest idea how to tell an Aberdeen Angus from the rest, I spoke to the auctioneer and asked him to point them out to me. He told me that they had bumps on their heads. I assumed that he was having a bit of a game with me, but he was being serious, and on closer inspection I could see that they did, indeed, have 'bumps' on their heads which differed from the shape of the others.

Two more feeble, scrawny looking calves you would have been hard put to find. After some considerable time, when most of the older cattle had been sold, the calves were wheeled in and sold in groups of fours and sixes. Finally in came the two pathetic looking Aberdeen Angus's barely able to put one hoof before the other, the white stickers bearing their numbers, together with the bumps on their heads, being the biggest part of them. For a minute I was in two minds as to whether to make a bid. I knew full well that if Chris had been in attendance there would be absolutely no chance of them accompanying us home. However, I felt so sorry for them that I decided that I would join in the bidding. Someone offered a paltry sum, followed by another bid. I then put my hand up and, lo and behold, the auctioneer promptly knocked them down to me. I did not know whether to feel pleased or not. Visions of Chris's reaction when he set eyes on them started looming in my mind, and my fears were not to go unjustified. He gave me the third degree as they hobbled up the lane to our barn, stopping every few paces to rest. He questioned my sanity, and flatly refused to have anything to do with them.

I had prepared their living quarters the previous day with a thick straw bed, and equipped the larder with calf milk powder, and calf rearing pencils just in case I bought them. The pencils are very small pellets of cow cake, and their size make it easy for calves to chew. In addition, I had an ample supply of top quality hay, and felt certain that I could transform them into well grown animals.

Twice daily, at 6am and 6pm, they were given warm milk, whisked up in a bucket on the floor of my kitchen and then driven up to the barn with me trying to avoid any bumps in the road so as not to slop it. Then their buckets were filled with calf pencils, and the hay-rack stocked up with the sweet smelling hay. After about a week there was a distinct improvement in their condition, and they were becoming quite lively.

The following spring I turned them out onto lush pasture, and felt positively proud of my efforts. They looked superb. Their coats were gleaming and they were enormous.

Christopher Cole, Philip's brother, had transported them back from Princetown for me, and happened to be passing and saw them in the field. He could not believe that they were the calves that he had off loaded a few months earlier and apologised for the derogatory remarks he had made about them, because, like Chris, he was not impressed at the outset, and had had grave doubts as to whether they would live, leave alone thrive.

We kept them for three years, when Polly was sold at Tavistock Market to a butcher, and Suki went into our freezer.

The Beer family from Uphill Farm, Yelverton.

Our first pigs – Pinky and Porky.

Porky's first litter.

A few of the sheep with their lambs.

Before the chop!

Christmas taken care of.

Chris plucking pheasants.

Philip at his Commissioning Parade.

Claire at her graduation ceremony.

Chris having his first experience as a jockey on Lincoln.

Chris with Tom at the Devon County Show.

Tom at Dunster with the castle in the background.

Myself on Tom, shortly after he had been 'backed'.

Albert pressing apples for cider.

Albert and Fred rolling out the barrels of cider.

Malcolm at the organ.

Aunt Rene with Ian and myself.

Chapter Fifteen

One day, my friend Glen was talking about a friend of hers. Angeline was on the same wave-length as Glen and I, keeping poultry and a Jersey house-cow. Glen invited me to go over with her to meet Angeline, and a suitable day was arranged for us to have lunch, and be introduced to Daisy.

Angeline was such a nice person, and made us very welcome. Daisy was beautiful with a very dark, brown face and huge brown eyes, and I fell in love with her on sight.

When Angeline and her husband decided to move, it was not possible for them to take the cow, and I was asked if I would be interested in having her. I was very keen, but wanted to be sure that Daisy could be milked by hand as I had noticed a milking machine in the parlour. I was assured that the animal was very quiet and would have no objection to being milked by hand. So a livestock haulier was asked to collect Daisy and deliver her to us one evening later that week.

The old, rickety chair that I had found when we cleared out the barn was resurrected, and its legs given a bit of a sort out to stop it wobbling. A large stainless steel bucket was bought off Eileen, and we were drooling at the thoughts of fresh, creamy milk in abundance. Daisy arrived bursting at the seams with milk, so into the barn she was ushered. She permanently wore a headcollar, so we threaded a piece of bale cord through the ring under her chin and tied her up, placing a trough of cow cake before her. Telling

h

her how lovely she was, I pulled up the chair, placed the bucket between my knees, took hold of the two teats that were nearest, and away I went across to the other side of the barn – chair, bucket, the lot. Feeling rather dazed, I got up and resumed my position under the cow. Up came the hind leg, and off I went again. Daisy was told that she was not lovely anymore, and details of what would happen to her if she did it again were spelt out in no uncertain terms. This made no difference whatsoever, and she did it again and again. We tried holding her tail up, then tried tying rope around her middle, all to no avail. Glen turned up with her son Stephen, and joined my husband and father. We all took a turn at milking in case it was my lack of technique that was causing the trouble. It had been a long time since I had milked Harry Rowlestone's cows, and I was out of practice, but we all got the same treatment, and were at a loss as to what to do next. Albert turned up. Seeing us all lined up beside Daisy, he asked, "How many does it take to milk a bloody cow?" but having heard an account of what happened each time an attempt was made, he did not volunteer to try, and shambled off. By now it was nearly dark, so we had to abandon the idea of a rice pudding, and decided that Daisy would have to go back to be machine milked or burst.

The haulier was re-contacted and asked to come straightaway. He was flabbergasted, having only just got home from delivering Daisy. I rang Angeline to tell her that we were on our way, but did not go into any details. Daisy was untied and driven back down the lane to the waiting lorry. Having ridden in it very recently, she was not keen to have another journey, and made it clear that she was not going without a struggle.

Some considerable time later, Daisy was incarcerated in the lorry, and Chris was frantically trying to wipe half a hundredweight of cow dung off the leg of his trousers with dock leaves. This had been Daisy's parting shot. My father was desperate for a pint, and told Chris to hurry up or they would not get a seat in the pub. Chris could not believe that his father-in-law was seriously expecting him to sit in the Leaping Salmon with cow dung trailing down his leg, but my father was serious, and was more concerned about his pint than the state of Chris's trousers. To compromise, Dad sat at the bar whilst Chris stood outside in the air, for which I am sure the other customers were truly grateful.

On arrival, Angeline's husband was looking positively murderous. I demanded that he milk the cow by hand in my presence. Into the parlour went Daisy. Down on a stool went Maurice. Up came Daisy's hind leg, and off went Maurice across the floor. He was livid. He grabbed a piece of rope, attached it to Daisy's tail, and hauled her up to a beam, so high that her back legs were off the ground. I was very upset, and told him that I was not in agreement with this barbaric practice, and suggested he use the machine. This being said, I drove off leaving Maurice in a foul temper, and poor Daisy swinging from the beams.

One often sees old photographs of men and women working in the fields on balmy, summer days, putting stooks of hay to dry, forking them up onto a cart, or constructing a rick. They are also pictured sitting down eating and drinking, and one gets the impression that they are enjoying every minute of their labour.

So taken in was I by this seemingly idealistic way of life, that I decided to give it a go. A stall in Tavistock Market sells bygone implements, and I had no trouble purchasing a vicious looking scythe as used by the folks in the old photographs. Then heading straight to my four acre field, looking every bit like the grim reaper, I set about scything down the grass. In less than ten minutes my hands were blistered, my back was breaking, and it had started to rain. Quite unlike the happy, smiling faces of the people in the photographs, I had a face like a hatchet, and a temper to match.

Flatly refusing to be beaten, I valiantly soldiered on despite having grave doubts about my sanity, and my ability to ever stand up straight again. On reflection, the workers in the photographs were somewhat bent and I was now beginning to see why. However, every cloud has a silver lining, and after much questioning as to why I had ever embarked on such an activity in the first place, I produced the sweetest smelling hay imaginable. It permeated the air, and could be smelt from some considerable distance away. The calves obviously enjoyed it as not one wisp was left to waste.

I struggle to work out how these people found time to do all this strenuous work in addition to all the other chores that had to be done. Today machines wash our clothes and do the dishes. Vacuum cleaners make light work of the cleaning, together with every conceivable type of chemical to make life easier, and yet we run around like headless chickens, never seeming to have enough hours in the day.

Despite the satisfaction of seeing my animals' obvious enjoyment of the produce of my not inconsiderable labours, I have not been tempted to repeat the exercise. When it has fleetingly crossed my mind to sharpen up the scythe and have another go, I have sat down and waited for the inclination to pass over. Instead, assistance is sort from local farmers who arrive equipped with tractors, cutters, turners and balers, doing the job in no time, leaving the skin on my hands, and in no need of physiotherapy.

The pleasure of feeding the hay made in this way as opposed to the old-fashioned method is nowhere near as satisfying, and the smell is no comparison. My hand-made hay had not been crushed by heavy, rubber tyres, sprinkled with drops of diesel, or contaminated by fumes, thus giving it the edge, and making it a far superior product. I dare not think what the wages bill would be if I employed someone to do what I did; if, indeed, I could find anyone daft enough to do it.

Men like Billy Butland and Frank Ridler are hard to find these days. They used to work for George Hillson who owned Knatham Farm in Yelverton. The work was back breaking, particularly at harvest time. Hay, straw, corn and potatoes had to be brought in and mangolds pulled, all without the benefit of modern day machinery.

All 'cottagers' kept a pig in those days and in addition to their wages each man was given a piglet as a bonus at the end of the harvesting. Billy and Frank placed their piglets in Hessian sacks and threw them over their shoulders in preparation for the walk home. They lived well over a mile from the farm, but hardly noticed the weight of the piglets at the outset of their journey. However, as they neared home, Billy was obviously beginning to feel the strain of the burden on his back and said to Frank, " 'Ere, my pig be growin', yer know."

Frank chided, " 'Ow d'ya make out that, you've fed it nought yet?"

"Well, ee be 'eavier now than when I picked ee up!"

Chapter Sixteen

Despite being determined to keep everything on a small scale, things inevitably began to escalate, and before we knew it, we were farmers rather than smallholders.

At the outset we were just going to have one of each animal, but needless to say, they tended to come in pairs. Pinky and Porky were next. They were collected for us by Albert who can only be described as a typical Westcountry farmer, and a real character. He was known from far and wide as he had rented land all over the place, and done business with most other farmers in the area. He was rather sceptical of us 'townies' at first, but soon realised we were not typical of town folk, and helped us considerably with all sorts of tasks. He could be quite scathing on occasions, and a good deal of shouting and swearing would take place, but we always ended up on good terms. He could also be quite embarrassing from time to time, not caring what he said, or to whom.

The lady who sold us the pigs was of rather large proportions. Instead of the usual greeting one would give a new acquaintance, he promptly told her she looked like a side of beef, and asked if she wore a Cross Your Heart bra, and if it was man enough to do the job. Having no mouse hole to go down, I had to quickly launch into conversation and drown any further derogatory remarks which were coming thick and fast. The lady, fortunately, seemed totally oblivious to the comments, and showed us the litter of piglets, of which she was justly proud. She assured us they were no trouble and invited us into the pen. As soon as the slightest gap was made in the door, they shot out like bullets from a gun. All there was to be seen was a pink streak disappearing across an allotment.

At this point, her husband appeared on the scene, not looking overly pleased. An altercation took place about being told not to open the gate, followed by a string of other do's and don'ts, followed by an estimate as to how long it was going to take him to get them all back. He was not the fittest looking of men, and seemed to wheeze a lot. On returning with the piglets following the bucket of nuts he was frantically shaking, he looked absolutely jiggered. How many revolutions of the allotment he had made was anyone's guess, but I got the impression from his hatchet-faced expression that it had been several. Finally we picked two gilts. They were three months old, pink and plump with lop ears. We were advised by Albert to go for lop-eared pigs as they could not see so much. This was a distinct advantage when trying to hoodwink them, which one has to do from time to time. A prick-eared pig is impossible to fool as it can see all that is going on around it, as our next pig, Pigatha was to demonstrate.

In preparation for the pigs' arrival, Chris once again set to work constructing stys, together with an exercise area.

No amount of advice on pigs can prepare you for the chaos they can cause. The stys were made of wood, as were the doors. The wooden partitions got eaten and the doors lifted off their hinges leaving the pigs free to ransack the place. It reminded me of the game of Monopoly when you have bought several houses and hotels for your properties, only to pick the dreaded card that tells you to make repairs on all of your houses.

When Pinky farrowed, we kept Pigatha and sold the rest of the litter at the market. This was a sad day, as all partings with our animals seemed to be, because we got so attached to them. However, most pig keepers appeared to be very pleasant people, so we felt assured that they would be happy until, that is, they met the butcher, but we refused to look that far ahead.

Getting three sows in pig proved to be a nightmare as AI is not that successful, so a boar needed to be found. Archie arrived; all goodness only knows how many stones of him. He was enormous to the point that he could hardly walk. I began to have grave doubts about his ability to 'do the deed'. However, all three pigs had litters thanks to Archie who was put down soon after, and will doubtless keep the nation in sausages for many years to come. This presented us with a problem when the sows needed serving again as there was not another local boar that we could borrow.

Finally we approached a couple who had bought a litter of piglets from us, and they agreed to let us run our sows with their boar when the time came. Roland was much smaller than Archie, and seemed to take quite a shine to Porky who was first to make his acquaintance. Having spent a pleasant afternoon with him, we loaded her back into the link box which was on the back of Albert's tractor, and made the three mile journey home.

On our arrival we discovered that Pinky had come into season, and was demanding an introduction to Roland. After a quick telephone call to the boar's parents, Porky was turned out, and Pinky loaded up, and off we went again. Unlike Porky, Pinky proved to be a bad traveller, and not long into the journey she decided to try and get out. This was very inconvenient as we were on the main Tavistock to Plymouth road which was busy at the time. The only thing to be done was to get the sow off her balance, as by this time her front legs were protruding over the side of the link box. The tractor had to be driven erratically in order to do this, so over the centre white line, then up the kerb we went for some considerable distance until Pinky had had enough of it, and her trotters disappeared back into the box. I decided that I could never face this trauma again, and resolved to buy my own boar.

Joshua was purchased from a dear old couple who had run a smallholding for many years, and despite being well into their eighties, were still keeping a few animals. They took great pride in their little farm with everything in pristine condition, including the old, grey Fergie tractor they used for an assortment of tasks. This tractor was their pride and joy, and had never let them down. I often think of them now. They put a lot of younger people to shame.

Once again, Albert came to our aid, and Joshua was loaded into his Suburu truck with an assortment of wood and old carpets lashed down over the top. Incredibly, Joshua was still in the truck when we got home. He turned out to be a really lovable pig. He was a Welsh X, and grew to be huge, with enormous tusks protruding from either side of his mouth making him look quite ferocious, but at no time was he spiteful. He loved his tummy rubbed, and would collapse at my feet, roll over onto his side, and stay there for as long as I would tickle him.

One day a litter of very tiny piglets escaped into the run where Joshua was eating some goodies, and I was concerned that he might take umbrage when one piglet went to take a bite out of a loaf that Josh was about to devour. However, he gently pulled the bread away from the piglet and the piglet ran off. Another time I arrived to find some piglets had escaped and were cuddled up to Joshua who was lying down totally unconcerned.

'Escaped' seemed to be the password in the pig house. If it was not one lot, it was two. It did not seem to matter how carefully we penned them in, they would find an exit. I would be constantly reminded of the poor 'side of beef' being admonished over her escapologists, and had to laugh.

Fortunately our smallholding is some distance away from neighbouring houses, unlike a lady who is affectionately known as Piggy Sue, who keeps pigs in an area of her back garden. Tilly, her Large White sow went missing on one occasion, and was found some considerable time later in the next door neighbour's sitting-room!

Chris finally got sick and tired of the constant ritual of repairing the stys, and we decided to move them to more secure accommodation, something bordering on Broadmoor. We beavered away building blockwork walls, blockwork feeding troughs, and doors lined with corrugated iron. Plastic windows were installed, and the overall effect was very pleasing. In went Pinky, Porky, Pigatha and Joshua into their individual stys, and all seemed well, that was until Chris looked over the top of the sty housing Pigatha. As previously mentioned, she was a prick-eared pig, and the minute she saw Chris's face appear, in one movement, she turned and jumped straight out through the plastic window. It looked like a cartoon of Desperate Dan in the *Beano*. At first Chris was livid as he had worked so hard to provide them with windows, but we ended up in hysterics. Meanwhile, Porky, although lop-eared, had discovered that she too had a window, and decided to take a look out, thus sticking both front trotters through the plastic.

We went home to locate the teapot; the cure for all ills and frayed tempers.

Poor Pinky was only to give birth to two litters before she died. Shortly before producing the second litter she seemed to be rather lethargic and unwell. During the early hours she gave birth to eight piglets followed by another four half an hour or so later. Most of the piglets died shortly after birth with the longest survivors not lasting the day. All the piglets looked under-nourished and were very tiny and frail. Pinky died soon after the last piglet was born, lying in an area of the barn that was not easily accessible. Needless to say, Albert was contacted, and arrived with his tractor and a length of heavy chain which we attached to Pinky's back legs in order to tow her out. A live pig can be troublesome to move, but a dead pig is even worse, and it was some considerable time before she was finally dragged out through the door.

Then came the dilemma as to what to do next. My suggestion was to dig a large pit, but Albert was adamant that this was out of the question, and insisted that the entire family would have to be burnt. Indira Gandhi had died a few days before Pinky, and a funeral pyre had been built for her, so it was decided that if it was good enough for the Indian Prime Minister's daughter, it was good enough for Pinky.

Albert had a considerable amount of wood lying around in his fields which was gathered together and stacked up. Pinky was unceremoniously heaved up onto the buckrake that protruded from the back of the tractor, together with the poor little piglets, and taken into the field opposite where the cremation was to take place.

Having got the pigs assembled on the pyre, Albert began having misgivings about burning her in case she should have been inspected by a vet. Being as Pinky was now at least four feet above the ground and doused in diesel, and had shown no signs of infection, in addition to the fact that all the other pigs were in good health, I was not prepared to hang about and promptly struck a match. Flames quickly engulfed the pyre and before long the entire village of Horrabridge was smelling of bacon, and a pall of black smoke rose up from the field. My feelings of distress turned to hunger as I inhaled this delectable smell.

Despite the inferno surrounding her, Pinky did not alter in appearance, and Albert became more and more agitated. He was convinced that someone was going to investigate the cause and source of the smell, and that we were staring prosecution in the face. Undeterred I threw on more wood and diesel, and gave the pig a prod with a long stick in the hope that if she rolled onto her side she would look less conspicuous. However, this strategy failed. The wood supporting the rear end of the pig collapsed, and Pinky sat up, thus resembling a begging dog. For Albert this situation was horrendous, and he proceeded to curse me up hill and down dale for prodding the pig. "Look at the bugger now, you should have left it be," he exclaimed as the pig continued to sit motionless whilst the flames licked around her. My anguish at losing Pinky could not quell my amusement at this hideous state of affairs, as the charred pig sat bolt upright in the midst of the flames that crackled in the melting fat.

It was two days before Pinky ceased to resemble a pig, and Albert could, once again, sleep at night, but it took all of four days to burn out completely.

Chapter Seventeen

One day I decided it would be a good idea to keep a couple of sheep in order to add a little variety to our diet. We were now self-sufficient in beef, pork and chicken, and a leg of lamb started to sound like a good idea for a change. Hence the arrival of Baabara and Baarbie.

They were two beautiful Suffolk crosses, owned by a friend. Having got them we did not have the heart to eat them, so borrowed a ram called Paddy instead. Paddy was a pure-bred Suffolk, and although he gave us dirty looks from time to time, never actually threatened us with violence, unlike Rambo who was to be borrowed on the next occasion. Rambo would go through his 'head down, and charge' routine the minute we entered the gate, which was rather disconcerting. Monty's broom handle seemed rather inadequate when faced with this horned creature from hell. We managed to stay in one piece, but his owner sustained a broken wrist on one occasion when trying to catch him. He did father some good lambs, however, so we forgave him, but not enough to consider borrowing him again.

Baabara had a lovely lamb which we named Catkin as she was born in March when the catkins were in abundance around the field. She was the image of her father with a lovely, almost white, fleece, and jet black face. Again, she was not for eating, and so the flock grew and grew. It is a miracle that we ever ate anything we produced. Naming them was definitely a mistake, and so I resolved not to name the ones due for consumption. This makes things a little easier, but I still feel a Judas on arrival at the abattoir.

Turkeys were my next venture. Poor Chris had really wanted a farm like he wanted a hole in the head, but he patiently hammered and banged away until a suitable house was made ready for their arrival. We travelled some considerable distance to get them, but it paid off as they grew into beautiful birds which were succulent and juicy when sampled on 25th December.

They looked a bit miserable at first, having been kept with numerous others in a large barn. They were mottled with pink and blue spots, these being applied as they were being sexed and de-beaked so as to know who had been done and who had not, quite important when you have a thousand or more running around together. Having been pampered in a large, airy pen for a few days, they soon improved. I would squat down and whistle to them, their favourite tune being the *Volga Boatman*, to which they would display their feathers, and try and fly up onto my back nearly flattening me. The male birds looked quite spectacular prior to the dreaded day when they had to be killed, and it seemed criminal to have to dispatch them, but no amount of pleading with Chris to 'just keep one' made an iota of difference.

The pulling of the leg strings was quite a fiasco until Albert got someone to make a suitable device for us to screw on the wall. Prior to this we had to use a fencing strainer which was very awkward causing us to vow never to do turkeys ever again. In fact, there was always something that we swore we would never do again, but we always relented and carried on.

Ducks were to be the next on the scene, and Quackers seemed ideal. He was white and plump, and seemed like the perfect accompaniment for orange sauce. However, once again our hearts ruled our heads, and someone else had the pleasure of his presence on their dining-room table as payment for a favour. Not to be daunted, I put a number of duck eggs in an incubator borrowed from Eileen, and duly produced sixteen ducklings. These were kept under a red lamp in our lounge. I insisted on drawing the curtains of an evening in case someone thought it was a 'knocking shop' much to the amusement of my family. One duck in particular was quite striking being jet black with a white collar round his neck. We called him The Vicar. When they had grown to a reasonable size, we installed them up the field. Twice daily The Vicar would lead the others down to the stream to bathe. This was quite something to watch as they waddled along in single file, always in exactly the same order. This continued every day for some weeks, and then when they were fully grown, they flew away. We were left speechless. Apart from The Vicar none had been named, and we were well and truly psyched up for the day of execution, but they were obviously clairvoyant and did a bunk just in time.

This was to be the end of my poultry production, and the incubator was returned to Eileen, and the red light put away.

Our dear friend Albert, was never far away, and was always there to help us whenever the need arose, which seemed like most of the time. He was so supportive and caring that at times I do not know what we would have done without him. If one of our animals was about to give birth, he was sure to be in attendance, and sat up all night with us to assist with lambing on many occasions. Although he is amply built, he is incredibly gentle and reassuring.

Every year Albert used to round up a group of children to help pick up 'windfall' apples for cider making. In order to redress the balance, I volunteered to help on one occasion and reported for duty at Callisham Farm, near Yelverton. Also doing his bit towards the apple collection was a little three-year-old boy whose elder brother and sister were helping. He trailed along beside me and on picking up an apple, would enquire as to whether it was fit to put into the bucket. The conversation went as follows:

"This one's got a hole in it. Is it all right?"

"Yes," I replied.

"This one's got a dent in it. Is it all right?"

"Yes," I replied.

When he said, "This one's got bullshit on it. Is it all right?" I said nothing!

Several hours and bucketfuls later, Albert drove down to Fred Serpell's at Upham Farm in St. Ive near Liskeard, where the apples were crushed before being mashed between layers of straw to enable as much fruit juice as possible to be extracted when being pressed. The cider was then placed in wooden barrels.

Having got the cider back, the barrels then had to be 'trigged up' in an area of Albert's barn that was reserved for the purpose, and a tap inserted into one of the barrels. This done, all the helpers would be offered a sample of this rough cider.

Albert had pint glasses lined up on a shelf that was covered in dust, cobwebs and rat droppings! The prospect of drinking from them was daunting to say the least. If anyone expressed their concerns, they were simply told to 'stream it out'. The only place in which to do this was the horse trough! Dripping with perspiration and feeling parched from wrestling the barrels into place, we gulped down the amber coloured liquid leaving us totally unconcerned as to the state of the glasses and feeling positively 'squiffy'!

He is very fond of poetry, although not all of his poems are printable! He used to deliver meat for the local butcher soon after passing his driving test, and on arrival at Mason's Gate, Sampford Spiney, would be invited in for a cup of tea by Mrs Maddock. The cottage was owned by Spooner's and West Devon Hunt, and was intended for the occupation of the huntsman. However, as Michael Howard, the huntsman lived in Huckworthy Lodge, the cottage was rented to the Maddock's. A cider mug sat on the mantelpiece bearing the words of this poem.

> *Let the wealthy and great roll in splendour and state,*
> *I envy them not I declare it.*
> *I eat my own lamb, my own chicken and ham,*
> *I shear my own fleece, and I wear it.*
> *I have lawns, I have bowers,*
> *I have fruit, I have flowers,*
> *The lark is my morning alarmer,*
> *So jolly boy's now,*

111

Here's Godspeed the plough,
Long life and success to the farmer.

Mr Maddock told Albert that when he could recite the poem without hesitating, he could have the cider mug, and within two weeks the mug was Albert's.

At haymaking time he would be there with his tractor, helping in any way he could. When all the baling was done, he would hitch up his trailer, and take all the bales up to our barn to be stowed away ready for winter. We had no equipment of our own as farming on such a small scale did not warrant tying money up in expensive machinery that would lay idle for the rest of the year, so we were dependant on Albert, plus the Cole family who farmed at Sampford Spiney. They are a lovely family, and have been most kind to us. Philip and his father, Bill, would come over at the drop of a hat if we were in difficulty with a lambing or calving, and every year they shear our sheep for free, and Christopher transports bullocks to the abattoir for us. We are so lucky to have such true friends.

Bill Cole and Albert are roughly the same age, and often regale us with stories of various things that have occurred over the years when farming was done the old-fashioned way, and life was tough. They also recount the lives of various village characters, one of whom was Jannie Reap. Jannie was the first person in Peter Tavy to own a telephone. One day, the village policeman was chatting away to him when the telephone started to ring. Jannie took no notice of it whatsoever, and continued with the conversation. "Your 'phone's ringing," said the policeman, "Aren't you going to answer it?"

"No," said Jannie. "Ee be yer fer me, I not be yer fer ee."

The same policeman's wife had given birth to a baby at around the time that Albert's wife had produced their first child. It was during the war when black marketing was rife. Albert had kept pigs and been a slaughterman for most of his life, in addition to his other farming activities. One night at around 9pm, he was illegally moving a dead pig from his farm back to his house using his new baby's pram for transport. As he neared his back gate he encountered the policeman coming towards him. "Got the little maid out late, Albert," he said.

"Yes," replied Albert, pulling the storm cover up even farther, "I best get on 'ome, the missus'll give me hell else."

Very few folks in Horrabridge owned a radio, and one day, Sampson Doney, one of the village characters, bought one. He met one of his neighbours on the bridge one morning who had also recently acquired a radio. "My radio give rain, what did yours give?" he asked. Looking amazed, the neighbour said that his radio had given rain as well.

Albert was always making us laugh, usually when we were getting anxious about an imminent calving or whatever. Many times he spoke of an old lady known to all in the village as Granny Carpenter. Granny used to make black puddings, and would wash the intestines required for the job in the little stream that ran through the village and passed her cottage. Unfortunately, the stream contained sewerage, so Granny would station a child upstream and get it to shout out, "Floater coming, Gran," then she would get a stick, and guide it away from the intestines. It seems she suffered no ill effects, and lived to a ripe, old age.

Another of Albert's recollections was that of a family living out on the moor that had an old kitchen range with an enormous stock pot hanging over the fire beneath. Every day something would be added to the pot, but it was never emptied or washed up. One day a team of threshers arrived to attend to the harvest, and each man was given a helping from the stock pot. Within a short space of time, they were all lined up along the side of the hedge suffering the consequences. I doubt that they ever forgot their encounter with the stock pot.

Also living on the moor were a brother and sister who ran a smallholding between them. Emily and Frank Skinner had farmed at Budghill for many years. The farm was on the moor near to Tavistock. The sister was a bad-tempered individual, and made her brother's life a misery. "The lazy bugger won't get out and milk the cow," she complained to Albert one morning. At this time Frank was eighty-six years old.

Every morning for breakfast Emily would have two slices of

bread spread thickly with golden syrup and cream. Albert was there one day watching her preparing her breakfast and said, "It'll kill ee yer know," to which Emily snapped:

"Get 'ome, it'll take more than that." She was obviously right and lived until she was ninety-six.

One day Frank did not come downstairs for his breakfast, but Emily did not bother to find out why, and it was not until he had failed to appear for three days that she looked in his room and found him dead in the bed.

Another brother and sister known to Albert were Ern and Em Cole. They farmed at Longash Farm, Merrivale. The farm was isolated and would be completely cut off in severe winter weather. Em, as she was known, would often be seen in the Merrivale pub smoking her pipe, and was quite a character.

Fulford, Perry and Spear were farm suppliers, and would send a traveller to the farm to collect orders. One very severe winter the traveller was marooned on the farm as a sudden heavy snowfall made the moorland road impassable. Em had prepared a rabbit pie for their dinner that day, and the traveller was given a small portion. Having eaten the meagre meal, he asked if he could have some more. Ern told him in no uncertain terms that he could not have any more as they were short of food, and would have to make the pie last. Bedtime came, and the traveller had to sleep with Em and Ern. They did not have a proper bed, but slept on the floor with hessian sacks for covering. During the night the dog started to bark, so Em told Ern to go outside and investigate. When he had gone, Em turned to the traveller and said, "Now's your chance." Quite what she had been expecting is unknown, but the traveller sprinted down the stairs, and helped himself to another portion of rabbit pie.

Albert came from a large family, having six brothers and three sisters. Every Sunday they would go to church with their parents, and one day, for some reason, they attended the Ebenezer Chapel in Bere Alston.

Mr Hancock was a baker in Bere Alston. He was of fairly small stature, and dressed like a tramp's batman. He used to preach in the Chapel from time to time, his opening words being; "Heavenly, far-ther, us be gathered yer in your presence," and would then proceed with the prayers. At the end of the service on this occasion he announced that, "The takings last Sunday amounted to two shillings, three penny half penny, and the praycher for next Sunday will be nailed on the door!"

Albert's sister, Bertha, was married to Reginald Doidge. Reg had a friend who was commonly known as a 'gooseberry farmer' due to the fact that he grew fruit and flowers. Mr Dawe was a very efficient farmer, but a bit 'simple'. On one occasion he had a stomach problem and consulted the doctor who prescribed some tablets. The doctor asked to see him again in three days time when he asked Mr Dawe if he had passed anything. "Yes, he said, I've just passed Reg Toll carrying a ladder!"

In addition to his slaughtering and farming activities, Albert would take on odd jobs such as tree-felling, hedging and anything else that paid reasonably well, and this led him to be introduced to a very refined lady who bred Arab horses. She employed him to muck them out when her usual stable hand was unavailable.

She was quite a character, and would sleep in the field under a hedge with her horses in the summer time, and was generally a bit eccentric.

When she became elderly, and unable to care for herself, Social Services were called in to assist her. A close friend of mine worked for this authority at the time and was asked to attend in order to put the old lady to bed, and to return in the morning to get her up. No one had warned my friend of the conditions that existed at the cottage, so when she walked into the lounge and found a horse standing there, plus a broody hen sitting in the hearth on a clutch of eggs, she was speechless.

Albert used to buy cattle from neighbouring farmers, and on one occasion arranged to collect half a dozen well-grown Friesian steers from Ivan Bolton who farmed near Chillaton. Ivan was a lovely man by all accounts and, like me, treated all his animals as if they were pets. Albert asked Ivan to be sure to put the bullocks in a shed ready for collection so that he would not have any bother rounding them up. Ivan assured him that the beasts were very quiet and always came to call. He said that they ate out of his hand, and that he could do anything with them. However, on Albert's insistence he put them in a shed prior to collection.

The shed was a rather flimsy affair with asbestos sheeting cladding the sides. Albert duly arrived with his policeman friend Pete Rouse, and together with Ivan, they approached the shed. Pete looked in at the cattle who promptly took fright and careered straight out through the back of the shed practically taking it with them. All that was left to do was laugh.

Chapter Eighteen

Now that our children had finished their university degrees; with Claire working in London for an insurance company, and Philip at Sandhurst pursuing an Army career, I felt the urge to take up my passion for riding again.

A beautiful, pure-bred Cleveland Bay was featured in my 'horsey' magazine, and caught Chris's eye. Although he has never had riding lessons, or been involved with horses, he does like them, and has had occasional rides on horses that I have owned, plus, he has accompanied me when we have been on holiday and booked rides at stables for gentle hacks. The fact that he always seemed to get a 'problem' horse never put him off, and even when he fell off he would just remount and carry on.

I felt it important that we both liked the look of whatever horse I acquired, and so as Chris had expressed an interest in the Cleveland Bay, I contacted the Cleveland Bay Horse Society who provided me with a list of breeders.

The old adage goes – never buy the first horse you see. Southbrook Phantom was the first horse I saw, and I have had him for some years now.

Tom, as he is known to his friends, is a pure-bred Cleveland Bay standing 17 hands, and can be as stubborn as a mule. When he was eighteen months old, Chris bought him for me as a present for my fiftieth birthday, and his training proved to be quite a challenge. However, within six months he was coming along well, and I decided to show him at Devon County Show in the Cleveland Bay class for two-year-olds.

After much grooming and plaiting he looked superb.

Clive Jenkin, a horse transporter from Lamerton, collected us in his horse box that was a very grand affair with ample room for horses, and thick padding to reduce any risk of injury which was just as well, because although we had no problem getting Tom into the lorry, once inside he decided to party, and did his version of the Can-can all the way to Exeter.

On arrival he was manic and barely controllable. Poor Chris was wearing a pair of boots that had hardly any mileage on them, and after walking Tom around for over an hour to settle him down, had severe bruising to all of his toes.

Whilst Chris limped around on the end of the lead rein, I found out which ring I was to perform in and got myself dressed up for the occasion. Chris hobbled back with Tom who by now had calmed down considerably. Between gritted teeth I gave the horse instructions as to what I wanted him to do, together with details of the consequences that would befall him if he did not do as he was told. I took hold of the lead rein and proceeded into the ring. Sensing my annoyance with him, he was beautifully behaved, and seemed to really enjoy himself. He won his class and was also awarded the Cleveland Bay Horse Society rosette for being the best horse overall.

This was to be the last time a class for pure-bred or part-bred Cleveland Bays was to be included at Devon County Show. However, each year there is a show in Minehead, held in the lovely grounds of Dunster Castle, where Tom continued to win rosettes until they, too, discontinued this particular class.

When Tom was three years old, I decided it was time to 'back' him. Being of rather large build myself, and not likely to 'bounce' quite as well as in my younger days, I asked Doreen Fell from Merrivale to do the honours for me. Doreen is a lovely person, and is excellent at training horses. Tom spent three weeks with her, and was no trouble at all.

When he returned I rode him everyday for about an hour, and soon discovered a very annoying trait. One minute he would be walking along as good as gold, only to suddenly stop and flatly refuse to budge. No amount of effort on my part would get him to move. Thinking that I had been out of the saddle for too many years and had lost my touch, in addition to being considerably older, I enlisted the help of a professional.

I arranged for a horse trainer to ride Tom on a weekly basis, incorporating schooling up on the moor, followed by a short hack, taking one hour overall. All went well to begin with whilst Tom led her into a sense of false security. Then, a few weeks later, he struck.

Up on the moor, miles from anywhere, Tom stopped dead. No amount of persuasion on her part could get him to budge. Getting no response, she kicked harder and harder. The crop was commissioned, and he received a tap behind the girth. Again nothing happened. The crop was applied with more force across his backside, still with no response from Tom. She dismounted and tried to lead him forwards to no avail. Trying to turn him to the right and then the left met with the same result. She attempted to push him backwards but might as well have been trying to push a bus. Tom did not budge. She remounted, by now all profession-alism had left her. She kicked, whipped and swore for all she was worth. Tom continued to remain stationary.

By now the poor girl was really concerned as there was not a soul around, nor a house for miles. Obviously sensing her distress, Tom decided to move and brought her home safely some two hours later, red-faced and perspiring profusely.

Much to my surprise, she turned up again the following week, this time with a whip in each hand, and spurs on her heels. Tom obviously got the message, and behaved impeccably.

To the reader's who are not au fait with horse training, I must stress that the additional 'aids' were not intended to inflict pain, merely to reinforce the rider's request for obedience.

Pure-bred Cleveland Bays are now classed as a rare breed, and I feel fairly certain that this is a consequence of their stubborn nature. They are frequently crossed with either a thoroughbred or an Irish Draft, but pure-breds are thin on the ground. This is sad as they are beautiful, and can excel in any discipline, but one can understand anyone's reticence at wanting to ride off, never to be seen or heard of again until the Cleveland Bay chooses to return.

One day, I was discussing Tom's behaviour with Lawson Vallance. Mr Vallance lives nearby together with his wife and one of his sons. He is a marvellous man who has farmed man and boy, and even now, in his eighties, he would put a lot of people to shame, including me.

I spoke with him about the problem I had with Tom, and he told me about a mare that his father had bred. The story went back many years when Lawson was a young boy, and Shire horses were used for all the farm work. Lawson's father bred and trained all his own horses, keeping seven Shires in all. They were all obedient and hardworking with the exception of one particular mare who would display similar behaviour to that of Tom.

One cold, wet day, Lawson and his brother were working in a field a fair distance away from the farmhouse with this mare when she decided to down tools as she was apt to do. They tried everything to get her to move, all to no avail. Cold, wet, tired and exasperated, they walked back to the farmhouse leaving the mare between the shafts of the cart, standing in the field.

It was customary for Lawson, together with his father and brother, to check all the horses at 10pm before retiring to bed. On arrival at the stable on this particular night, the father immediately spotted the mare's absence. Lawson and his brother had completely forgotten about her. Their father blew his top and told them to go and bring her in, and dared them to leave her until she was bone dry, fed and watered.

Next day, the mare was once again put between the shafts and driven down to the fields where she worked hard and long, giving them no trouble whatsoever, and continued to do so from that day on. She had clearly learnt her lesson, as did another of their horses who objected to being tied up.

Every horse had a stall, and was tied up with a length of rope that had a wooden ball on the end. The rope was fed through a ring, and enabled the horse to lie down. This particular horse would come in and be tied up. He would eat his food, and then violently fling back his head, breaking the rope in the process, and would then run off. Time after time this happened, then one night Mr Vallance tied him up with a length of cotton. He ate his food; flung back his head, fell over backwards, and never did it again.

I am still trying to find a cure for Tom, but he has improved as he has become more mature, which is better than nothing, and as our relationship is like a marriage, being for better or worse until death do us part, it appears that I am stuck with it.

Chris and I remain self-sufficient in meat, and I continue to live as if I am going to die tomorrow, and farm as though I am going to live forever.

Epilogue

As I stated in the very beginning, I feel so privileged at having been part of a close-knit family, but I am also extremely grateful to my parents and family for the time they devoted to talking to me and my brothers about events that had occurred over the years. Instead of sitting silently in front of a television set, we chatted and reminisced, and this has enabled me to write this book, thus preserving these memories not only for my children, but hopefully for other people totally unrelated to me to enjoy.

So much is lost by not talking about past events, as so often happens. Sadly, parents and relatives die, and their stories go with them to the grave. Philip has expressed his regret at not having asked my father more questions, and I regret not having delved more deeply into my maternal grandmother's history, but now it is lost forever.

I hope this book inspires others to follow the example of my parents and talk to their children. So much fun and laughter comes out of sitting around the fire chatting, and it draws everyone closer together. Problems get aired and disputes settled, leaving everyone feeling better and more united.